MW00776384

IMAGES
of America

URBANNA

The commercial waterfront on Urbanna Creek can be seen as the two-masted schooner *Manaway* lies anchored on the creek. *Manaway* was owned by J.W. Hurley of Urbanna and was lost at sea in 1924 when a menhaden fish steamer ran into her in a thick fog and cut her in two. She was bound for Baltimore with a load of canned tomatoes. (Courtesy of Emily Chowning.)

On the Cover: The Ross House Hotel was owned by W.C. "Captain Billy" Fitzhugh when this launch, *Gentry*, was used to pick up passengers, mail, and freight off steamboats unable to enter Urbanna Creek. Early steamboats did not have reverse gear and were difficult to maneuver inside creeks, so vessels often moored in the river, and launches like the *Gentry* were used to access them. (Courtesy of Emily Chowning.)

Larry S. Chowning

ISBN 978-1-5316-6239-4

Published by Arcadia Publishing
Charleston, South Carolina

Library of Congress Control Number: 2011941842

For all general information, please contact Arcadia Publishing:
Telephone 843-853-2070
Fax 843-853-0044
E-mail sales@arcadiapublishing.com
For customer service and orders:
Toll-Free 1-888-313-2665

Visit us on the Internet at www.arcadiapublishing.com

As an Urbanna native, I would like to express heartfelt gratitude to the late Cora Marchant, Charles "Charlie" Henry Palmer Jr., and Robert "Bob" and Elizabeth Bristow, all of whom lived on Watling Street, where I have spent my life. When I was a boy, they shared their love of Urbanna and its history in slower times when I stopped by for a glass of lemonade and a trip to the front porch swing to sit and talk. Thank you for enriching and nurturing my love of history and my life.

CONTENTS

ACKNOWLEDGMENTS

I want to thank all those who have assisted me in this effort to produce a photographic history book of the town of Urbanna. Without your help, this would not have been possible. I also want to thank the Urbanna Tricentennial History Committee, co-chaired by Jessie Martin DeBusk, Stuart Chewning, and author Evelyn Q. Ryland who in 1980, published *Urbanna—A Port Town in Virginia 1680–1980*. Her work was paramount in assisting me in this project. I want to thank owners Fred and Betty Lee Gaskins and editor Tom Hardin of Urbanna's *Southside Sentinel* for providing me with an avenue to write in my hometown. The following organizations and groups were instrumental in the creation of this work: the Urbanna Masonic Lodge No. 83, the Middlesex County Public Library, the *Southside Sentinel*, the Middlesex County clerk's office, the town of Urbanna, and the Library of Virginia. Individuals who provided valuable information and photographs are Carroll C. Chowning Sr., Betty and Carroll C. Chowning Jr., Emily and H.S. "Shep" Chowning Jr., Dee Chowning, Hannah Chowning, Kevin Barrick, Bonnie Williams, Bob and Carolyn Henkel, Buddy Davis, Burton and Elizabeth Leaf, Virginia Burton, Betty Burton, William C. Hight, Seldon Richardson, Dr. A.L. VanName, Terry Murphy, Joe Cardwell, George Mills, Davis Wilson, Wit Garrett, Jonesey Payne, L.M. and Albert Carlton, Walt Hurley, Roy Bowman, Richard Marshall and his mother Lucy, John Segar, Joe Conboy, Dick Murray, Mary Kay Hight and her mother Louise Mercer, J.W. Dunn, J.D. Davis, Grace Daniel, David Cantera, Margaret Gerdts, Anne Wheeley, Elizabeth Richardson, Beth Maxwell, Douglas Taylor, Vera and John England, Julie Burwood, Joe Gaskins, Judy and Don Richwine, Archie Soucek, Beatrice Taylor, Ann Wheeley, Betty Shelton, Sam Richardson, and Ed Starbird. I also wish to thank Arcadia Publishing acquisitions editor Brinkley Taliaferro Gary for her expert guidance and her appreciation of the history of Tidewater, Virginia, as her ancestral roots are in Essex County, Virginia.

INTRODUCTION

Urbanna was founded in 1680 as an English Colonial port of call with a deepwater creek, providing easy access for the on- and off-loading of commercial goods. Native American arrowheads, spearheads, and million-year-old mollusk shells found along the creek bank are reminders that life existed here before the arrival of the English.

Urbanna was in the middle of a huge body of water called the Calvert Sea approximately 20 million years ago, and shells from that period can be found along the shores on the Rosegill side (south side) of Urbanna Creek. In 1929, paleontologist Wendell C. Mansfield of the US Geological Survey visited Urbanna Creek and discovered several new species of shell, two of which he named *Carolinapecten urbannaensis* and *Marvacrassatella urbannaensis* after the town of Urbanna. These fossil shells indicate life in the area long before Middlesex Indians or English settlers ever set foot here. The fossil beds along the creek and on the riverbanks of Rosegill are predominantly from the Miocene Epoch (5–23 million years ago).

Archaeological research has found evidence of middle (2,500–1,000 years ago) to late (1,000–400 years ago) Woodland Indian habitation at several locations on the former Rosegill plantation across the creek from Urbanna. Native Americans resided on the Rosegill and Urbanna tracts of land from 10,000 years ago through the 18th century. When soldier and adventurer Capt. John Smith completed his famous 1612 map of Chesapeake Bay, he noted there was an Indian town then located on the high banks of what was to become Urbanna Creek. They were Algonquian-speaking Indians of Virginia, part of the Powhatan tribe that was ruling the local area in 1607 when the English arrived at Jamestown. In 2010, the state of Virginia placed a historical highway marker just before the bridge entering town as a tribute to John Smith's so-called mystery village. The marker states, "In 1608, Captain John Smith mapped Opiscopank near here as an Indian town where a chief lived."

Several years after Smith's explorations, Indians known as Nimcocks were living on the creek. On June 16, 1649, two former villages were identified in a grant to Capt. Ralph Wormeley for 3,200 acres that became Rosegill Plantation. The grant states, "On the s. side of Rappahannock River, about 10 miles up the river, including the Indian Townes, old & new Nimcock." This was the first and only time Nimcock Indians were mentioned during that period other than references to Nimcock Creek as a name for Urbanna Creek in English grants. Another Indian name that has survived into modern times is that of the Rappahannocks, a tribe that lived on the north side of the river. The Rappahannock River is named for them, and the town's northern boundary runs along the river.

The town's eastern and southern boundaries are defined by Urbanna Creek. The western boundary is marked by a small creek officially known as Perkins Creek but locally called the Little Creek. Bertram Obert achieved a patent for the land along the western boundary on November 16, 1650. Obert Street, named for him, runs from Rappahannock Avenue to a bluff overlooking Perkins Creek.

Early setters came to Virginia in search of gold and treasures, but finding none, they soon turned to the land to make a living. In 1612, John Rolfe introduced Virginia to tobacco, which grew into the money crop of the colony. The tobacco trade was further enhanced when Virginia planters began experimenting with a South American tobacco seed. A sweet-scented brand extremely popular in England, this tobacco grew best in the type of soil found along the banks of Tidewater's rivers and creeks, including the Rappahannock River and Urbanna Creek. In the 1620s, the rising price of tobacco brought hundreds of new colonists into Virginia seeking their fortune. Over the next 50 years, Virginia's economy was driven by the tobacco business.

Urbanna's origin goes back to June 1680, when the Virginia Assembly's Act of Cohabitation encouraged the establishment of 19 tobacco port of entry towns throughout the Virginia colony. The act specified that each county set aside 50 acres for a port and market town. The British wanted to encourage people to move to Virginia, realizing a diverse economy with centrally located centers of commerce was needed to create jobs and opportunities beyond growing tobacco. The greatest opponent of the town was Ralph Wormeley II of Rosegill.

Wormeley gladly accepted 10,000 pounds of tobacco for 50 acres of his land, but immediately fought the notion of allowing a town across the creek from his Rosegill and refused to sign paperwork for the sale. When local officials decided to survey the lots in town without Wormeley's official approval, he sent slaves and others to discourage the progress. He was successful. For a while, the matter of creating a town was put on hold, but Wormeley's death in 1701 opened the door again. On October 23, 1705, the Assembly in Williamsburg officially created a town in Middlesex County: "Whereas several laws have appointed and confirmed unto the county of Middlesex 50 acres of land for a town." The town was officially named Urbanna, meaning "City of Anne" in Latin, for the reigning Queen Anne of England in 1706.

Middlesex County Courthouse was moved to town in 1748 when a brick structure was built to provide a home for the county court system. It remained the county seat of Middlesex until it was moved to Saluda in 1852, after a bitter dispute. Located in Urbanna for 104 years, the small, Colonial courthouse, which still stands today, was the site of dynamic changes in Urbanna and in America. It was there that the "Middlesex Resolutions" were drafted and first read to the public as a warning to the British that Urbanna and Middlesex County would not tolerate taxation without representation. The issue of freedom of religion was the topic of debate in 1771, when Baptist minister John Waller and other local Baptists were imprisoned in the Urbanna "gail" because they had no license to preach. Waller preached from the jailhouse window, and the Baptist faith spread like wildfire throughout the region.

The town prospered during the Colonial period as tobacco trade brought commerce from England and elsewhere, and farmers brought their tobacco to town to be inspected and registered at the customhouse. But by 1852, Urbanna was no longer an international port of call, and the slow-moving chain ferry across the creek irritated those trying to reach town on county court days. At a busy crossroad five miles from Urbanna, a group from the Saluda area was able to bring the matter of moving the courthouse out of town through an approved voter referendum. Legend has it the referendum was approved by one vote, cast by a dying man who was brought to the polls on a cot by proponents of the Saluda site.

Urbanna was raided and pillaged during the Revolutionary War and the War of 1812, and bombarded and occupied by Union troops during the Civil War. Just prior to American victory at Yorktown, the town was raided by the British in 1781. "Thirty-five or forty" British privateers went ashore at Urbanna and Rosegill, plundering the town and plantation. In retaliation, Hugh Walker of Urbanna raised a small force to attack the ship and presented enough of a challenge that the British sailed away.

During the War of 1812, Essex and Middlesex Counties' militias saved Urbanna from the British. In December 1814, two captured British soldiers told local militias of a plan to burn the town. Legend has it that when militiamen and townspeople learned of this, they constructed fake cannons and mounted them atop the hill in clear view of the river. When the British approached the mouth of Urbanna Creek, soldiers and citizens congregated around the cannons, giving the impression that they were getting ready to fire upon the fleet. The Urbanna artillery actually consisted of one real cannon, which was fired to further give the impression to the British that if they were going to invade the town they were going to be in for a fight. The British had over 500 troops on the ships, many more than the Americans had standing atop the hill on Urbanna Creek. Unwilling to face unknown odds, however, the British sailed away and out of the Rappahannock River. The location of the staged artillery is called Fort Nonsense to this day.

During the Civil War, Urbanna's deepwater harbor was a strategic location for Union and Confederate authorities. In December 1861, Major Gen. George B. McClellan designed a back door plan for an offensive thrust against Gen. Robert E. Lee's rebel army perched along the Manassas line. The Union general decided to load his army on transports, cruise to Urbanna, and use the creek to off-load troops behind Lee's army to capture Richmond, the Confederate capital. Winter weather conditions stalled the plan, and McClellan decided to wait until spring. In the meantime, Pres. Abraham Lincoln was growing impatient with lack of aggression on the part of General McClellan, and on January 27, 1862, Lincoln ordered an advance of all Union armies to begin February 22. Lincoln's order surprised McClellan, who immediately went to the commander-in-chief with his "Urbanna Plan" in hand. Lincoln objected to the plan because he, and others, felt it would leave Washington, DC, open to Confederate attack. On March 8, Lincoln had McClellan submit the plan to his 12 division commanders who voted 8 to 4 in favor of the Urbanna route to Richmond. The town was saved when the Confederate army abandoned the Manassas line, and Urbanna was no longer a strategic location for the Union army.

Throughout the war, Urbanna Creek was a staging ground for both Federal and Confederate activities, and from time to time camps were set up in town. Union ships were coming and going, offering instant freedom for slaves willing to fight for the Union. After a Rappahannock River maritime battle in the summer of 1863, planned and carried out by Confederate president Jefferson Davis's nephew John Taylor Wood, Rosegill Plantation house was transformed into a hospital, where wounded Union, Confederate, and former slaves were treated.

After the Civil War, New York and New Jersey oystermen came south to harvest and purchase oysters to feed the population centers of the North. Oysters were a staple food for northerners and had been since the late 1700s. The Chesapeake Bay and Rappahannock River were loaded with oysters. Urbanna's deepwater harbor was ideal for large oyster boats, and an economy based on oysters grew in the town. Come October 1 of each year, oystermen from throughout the region and Tangier Island came to Urbanna to harvest oysters. This industry was a major part of the town's economy from 1880 to the 1960s. As disease and over-fishing slowed the industry, the community established the Urbanna Oyster Festival in 1961 to highlight the role oysters played in the economy of the town. The festival grew from a small local affair drawing a few thousand people, to today's two-day festival attended by over 60,000 people. In 1988, the Virginia General Assembly voted to make the Urbanna Oyster Festival the official oyster festival of the commonwealth of Virginia.

Today, the 600 or so people who live in the incorporated limits of Urbanna are on sacred ground, where Native Americans, British Tories, American Patriots, slaves and masters, and Union and Confederate troops once trod. The town has been center stage in the growth and development of this country as one of the first Southern English towns established in America.

One

Before a Town

Urbanna is located in Middlesex County, Virginia, a 40-mile stretch between the Rappahannock and Piankatank Rivers, with Chesapeake Bay at the far eastern end of the county. Issued on July 20, 1642, the first Middlesex County English land grant was given to John Matrum for 1,900 acres on the Piankatank River. An Indian uprising in 1644 forced English settlers on the frontier to move back to the north bank of the York River. In 1649, permanent settlement began in the county, and that year Capt. Ralph Wormeley received a land grant for Rosegill Plantation, including land that would later become Urbanna. Wormeley died shortly after receiving the grant. Deputy governor of the Virginia Colony Sir Henry Chicheley, who married Captain Wormeley's widow, then occupied the Rosegill Plantation. The deputy governor was instrumental in shaping political, social, and religious life in the county.

Through Chicheley's efforts, the main Anglican church, Christ Church, was located a short distance from Rosegill. The Glebe, home to the minister, was built at the head of Urbanna Creek near Chicheley's plantation. The county court was first established on what was to become Town Bridge Road (leading into town) and later, at Stormont, not far from Rosegill. The Anglican church and court system were important elements in creating a society similar to what the colonists had left behind in England. The proximity of a town to the church and courthouse was part of the reason that, in 1680, the Virginia Assembly considered land near Rosegill as a site for a town. The main reason for the location, however, was the deepwater creek with high sloping banks, an ideal British port of call on the south bank of the Rappahannock River. Just over 50 years after permanent settlement, Middlesex County got a town—Urbanna.

On June 16, 1649, Capt. Ralph Wormeley received a patent for 3,200 acres, 50 of which would become the town of Urbanna on Nimcock Creek. The Wormeley family owned Rosegill Plantation until the early 1800s. (Courtesy of Betty Chowning.)

Christ Church, located just a few miles outside of Urbanna, was established in 1666 as the mother church of Middlesex County. Part of the Anglican Church of England, Christ Church was state sponsored and was attended by the people of Urbanna exclusively until 1770, when the Baptist movement arrived in Middlesex County and Urbanna. (Courtesy of Betty Chowning.)

Located on Town Bridge Road, the Glebe was the residence of ministers for Christ Church Parish from its beginning until the disestablishment of the church following the Revolutionary War. The photograph above shows the last structure, built by members of the Anglican Church, completed in 1757. The Glebe burned to the ground in 1913. (Courtesy of Betty Chowning.)

The Colonial plantation of Hewick is located just west of town. Christopher and John Robinson of Hewick and Harry Beverley of Brandon Plantation are called the "fathers of Urbanna," as the three men petitioned the Middlesex County court in 1704 to appoint them officers to create a town. After the Port Act was approved by the Virginia Assembly in 1706, the town was officially named Burgh of Urbanna. (Courtesy of Betty Chowning.)

This early Colonial kitchen was worked by slaves for as long as the Wormeley family owned Rosegill. When Capt. Ralph Wormeley obtained the Rosegill Plantation on June 16, 1649, he was given an additional 3,200 acres, which were divided into parcels of 50 acres for each of the 64 people he paid to transport from England. Wormeley's grant also included "eight Negros—transported in Capt. Jon. William Shipp," along with nine other slaves. (Courtesy of Emily Chowning.)

Two

Colonial Village

Urbanna Creek was an ideal port of call for the colony's tobacco trade. Tobacco was grown in the county and delivered to town in wooden barrels called "hogsheads," which held 1,000 pounds of leaf tobacco. The sloped hills allowed gravity to aid in moving hogsheads down to the wharfs. During the Colonial period, the road down to the water, now Virginia Street, was called Prettyman's Rolling Road.

The Assembly's Warehouse Act of 1730 established Urbanna as the "official inspection station" of tobacco for Middlesex County, further ensuring the town's position as a major center of commerce in the region. Ships from England and the West Indies arrived frequently in the creek, and Scottish factors established retail and general merchandise stores.

By 1743, there was a bridge over the head of the creek on what is now Town Bridge Road. When the courthouse came to town in 1748, a private ferry crossing the creek from Rosegill was made a public ferry. By 1769, Urbanna was one of six "official" ports of call on the Rappahannock River, where tobacco had to be brought, inspected, and graded. In 1769, a total of 31 schooners, 23 ships, 13 brigs, 12 sloops, and six snows frequented the river ports. There were 11,765,088 pounds of produce exported from these six ports and shipped to England, Europe, and the West Indies.

Built in 1748, the Middlesex County courthouse was one of 11 Colonial courthouses still in existence in Virginia, listed with the Virginia Historic Landmarks Commission and in the National Register of Historic Places. Although it was modified in the 1850s to accommodate church facilities, the courthouse is a reminder of Urbanna's Colonial heritage, when the town was the county seat of Middlesex County. (Courtesy of Emily Chowning.)

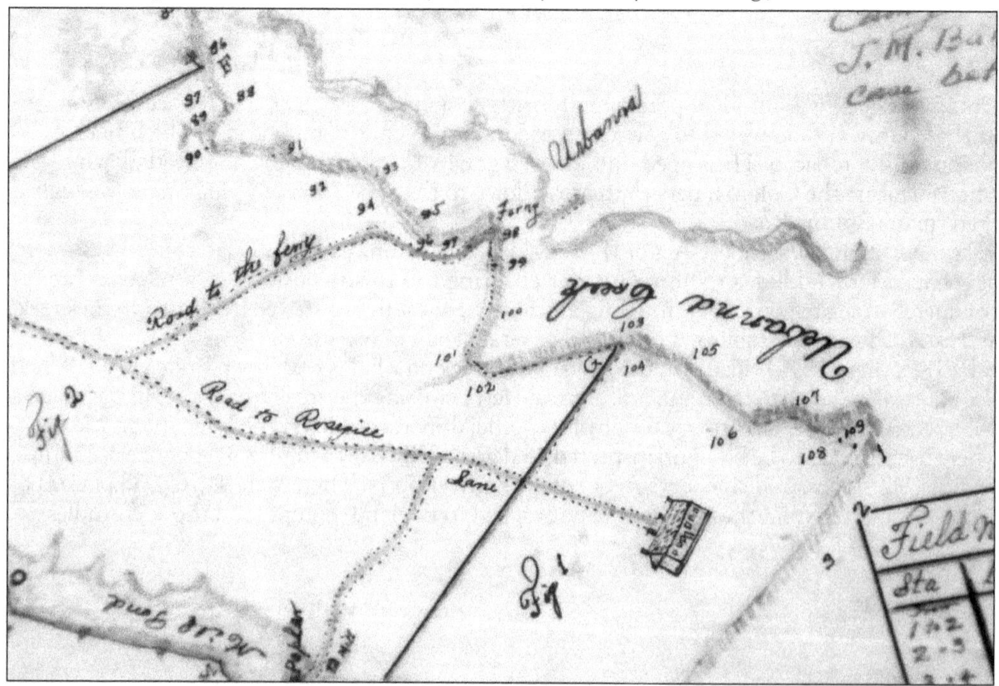

This survey plat shows the "road to the ferry," Rosegill Plantation, and Rosegill Mill. The mill was the main provider of white and yellow corn meal and wheat for town residents in the 17th and 18th centuries. The mill was moved across the creek and into the town in 1909, becoming Middlesex Manufacturing Co. (Courtesy of Middlesex County Clerk's Office.)

Tobacco was graded and priced for shipment to England at the Colonial Customhouse on Virginia Street. The structure is believed to have been built between 1754 and 1762 by John Gordon. The customhouse was bought in 1934 by former governor of Virginia Andrew Jackson Montague and is owned today by his relatives. (Courtesy of Middlesex County Public Library.)

The restored James Mills Scottish Factor Store or "Old Tobacco Warehouse" is used as the town visitor's center today. For years, it was thought to have been used to store hogsheads of tobacco. In 1958, the Association for the Preservation of Virginia Antiquities sponsored a study of the building. Historian Wesley Newton Laing's research revealed that the structure was not a warehouse but, rather, a Scottish Colonial merchant factor store, where tobacco could be traded for finished goods from Europe. (Courtesy of Emily Chowning.)

Lansdowne (above) was built around 1740 as a summer home for the Wormeley family of Rosegill. Dr. Arthur Lee purchased Lansdowne in 1791 and is buried in the cemetery behind the home. During the American Revolution, Lee, along with Benjamin Franklin and Silas Deane, negotiated the Treaty of Alliance with France in 1778, a key element in the eventual victory over the English. Lee also owned the Wormley-Lee-Montague Cottage (below), the oldest wood frame house still standing in Urbanna. Built around 1748, the house has been home to many families. It was in great disrepair in 1976 when Robert Latane Montague III of Alexandria and Urbanna bought the house and restored it. The cottage is listed on the register of Virginia Historic Landmarks. (Courtesy of Betty Chowning.)

The Colonial tavern or "ordinary" served as a boardinghouse and pub on Prince George Street. The tavern also was a place for dancing, fiddling, and drink or "tipple." George Chowning and Benjamin Rhoads obtained a business license in 1765 to operate the tavern "in the sum of Fifty Pounds current Money." The county court ordered that they provide "wholesome and cleanly Lodging and Diet for Travellers and Stableage, Fodder and Provender as the Seasons shall require for their horses." Also, "unlawful Gaming in the House . . . nor on the Sabbath Day suffer any person to tipple . . . any more than necessary" was not allowed. The Colonial county court set prices for beverages served there. In 1770, tavern keepers served Canary wine, Malaga, sherry, Madeira wine, Claret, Rhenish, Fyall wine, Nants, French brandy, Arrack, Caribbean rum, Virginia brandy, beer, and apple cider. (Courtesy of Middlesex County Public Library.)

During the Revolutionary War, Ralph Wormeley V of Rosegill was a well-known Tory and a member of Lord Dunmore's Virginia Council. His strong sympathies towards the English government in Virginia caused him to become a target of concern for American patriots, who considered Rosegill a Tory stronghold. (Courtesy of Middlesex County Public Library.)

Hampstead, three miles west of Urbanna, was once the home of Henry Washington around 1750. A cousin of Pres. George Washington, he served on the vestry at Christ Church Parish and is buried in the cemetery of Bruton Parish in Williamsburg. The Colonial gristmill, once part of Hampstead, served Urbanna and the surrounding areas until the late 1940s. (Courtesy of Betty Chowning.)

Three

Civil War and the Days of Sail

The Revolutionary War brought an end to Urbanna's era of international trade. The war split the community right down the middle, with patriots and Tories living side by side. Rosegill's Ralph Wormeley V was banished for a while to southwest Virginia for his Tory sympathies, while the Middlesex (patriot) Committee convened at the town courthouse over those committing pro-English actions.

When the war ended, the nation was in a deep recession. The British made things even worse during the War of 1812 by plundering and raiding Urbanna. The freight sailing vessel business helped the town dig out of the recession, as townsmen became sailing captains and mates. Some owned and operated their own boats. The era of sailing schooners lasted from the 1830s to the late 1940s. New York and New Jersey oystermen in large sailing vessels began coming to Urbanna in the 1830s, buying oysters locally and stimulating the economy. By 1860, Urbanna's economy had rebounded to some extent, but the Civil War brought an end to those few years of prosperity.

The slave population in Middlesex County and Urbanna was larger than the ruling white class. Townspeople never forgot Nat Turner's slave rebellion in 1831 in nearby Southampton County that resulted in the deaths of 60 white men, women, and children. Around the time when abolitionist John Brown unsuccessfully attempted to organize slaves to mount a revolt, townsmen organized the "Middlesex Light Dragoons." On June 2, 1861, the dragoons were reorganized as the Confederate Company C of the 55th Virginia.

During the Civil War, Harriette Smith lived at the Glebe. Union gunboats chased a confederate vessel, *Bloomer*, up Urbanna Creek, and Confederate Hiram Carter ran his vessel into shallow water near the Glebe. The Smith family helped Carter unload his possessions, helped him set the boat on fire so the Yankees would not capture it, and hid Carter somewhere on their farm. When Union sailors saw the boat in flames, they did not pursue Carter. As a token of his appreciation, Carter gave the Smith family a brown earthenware pitcher. Carter's pitcher is now a treasured Smith family heirloom. (Courtesy of Betty Chowning.)

Union troops occupied the town when this drawing of a Yankee camp was published in *Harper's Weekly*. Urbanna is visible in the background. (Courtesy of Selden Richardson.)

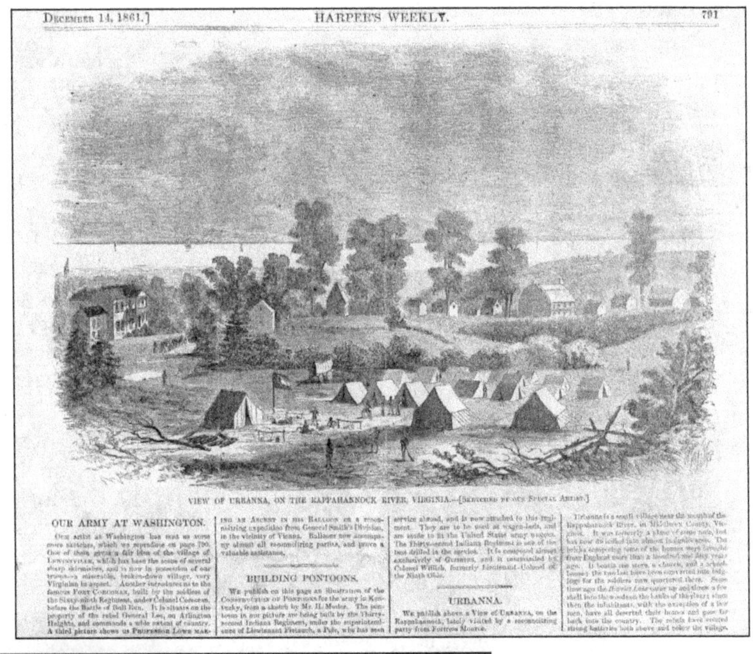

DECEMBER 14, 1861.] HARPER'S WEEKLY. 791

VIEW OF URBANNA, ON THE RAPPAHANNOCK RIVER, VIRGINIA.—[SKETCHED BY OUR SPECIAL ARTIST.]

OUR ARMY AT WASHINGTON.

OUR artist at Washington has sent us some more sketches, which we reproduce on page 790. One of them gives a fair idea of the village of LEWINSVILLE, which has been the scene of several sharp skirmishes, and is now in possession of our troops—a miserable, broken-down village, very Virginian in aspect. Another introduces us to the famous FORT CORCORAN, built by the soldiers of the Sixty-ninth Regiment, under Colonel Corcoran, before the Battle of Bull Run. It is situate on the property of the rebel General Lee, on Arlington Heights, and commands a wide extent of country. A third picture shows us PROFESSOR LOWE MAKING AN ASCENT IN HIS BALLOON ON A RECONNOITRING expedition from General Smith's Division, in the vicinity of Vienna. Balloons now accompany almost all reconnoitring parties, and prove a valuable assistance.

BUILDING PONTOONS.

WE publish on this page an illustration of the CONSTRUCTION OF PONTOONS for the army in Kentucky, from a sketch by Mr. H. Mosler. The pontoons in our picture are being built by the Thirty-second Indiana Regiment, under the superintendence of Lieutenant Fleisauch, a Pole, who has seen service abroad, and is now attached to this regiment. They are to be used as wagon-beds, and are made to fit the United States army wagons. The Thirty-second Indiana Regiment is one of the best drilled in the service. It is composed almost exclusively of Germans, and is commanded by Colonel Willich, formerly Lieutenant-Colonel of the Ninth Ohio.

URBANNA.

WE publish above a View of URBANNA, on the Rappahannock, lately visited by a reconnoitring party from Fortress Monroe.

Urbanna is a small village near the mouth of the Rappahannock River, in Middlesex County, Virginia. It was formerly a place of some note, but has now dwindled into almost insignificance. The bricks composing some of the houses were brought from England more than a hundred and fifty years ago. It boasts one store, a church, and a school-house; the two last have been converted into lodgings for the soldiers now quartered there. Some time ago the *Harriet Lane* came up and threw a few shell into the woods on the banks of the river; since then the inhabitants, with the exception of a few men, have all deserted their homes and gone far back into the country. The rebels have erected strong batteries both above and below the village.

This portrait of Sgt. William X. Smith of Urbanna in his Confederate uniform hangs on the wall of the Middlesex County historical courtroom. Smith was shot at the Battle of Chancellorsville, the same day Stonewall Jackson was shot. When Jackson was shot, Urbanna doctor Richard Allen Christian was standing a few yards from the incident, and assisted the wounded general, who eventually died. (Courtesy of Middlesex County Circuit Court.)

During renovations to the Middlesex County Courthouse in 1913, a cannonball was found lodged in a rafter. At that time, Carroll C. Chowning Sr. was invited into the attic of the courthouse to examine the cannonball. Chowning discovered the following etched in pencil right beside it: "Court House in Urbanna was bombarded by the Federal fleet consisting of a tug and steamer on November 8, 1861." This discovery inspired Chowning to research, record, and preserve the untold history of Urbanna. (Courtesy of Betty Chowning.)

OATH AND PAROLE.

No 79

Office of Provost Marshal,

~~Richmond~~ Urbana, Va., May 22 1865.

I George W. Smith, Citizen of Middlesex Co. Va. do solemnly swear, in the presence of Almighty God, that I will henceforth faithfully support, protect and defend the Constitution of the United States, and the Union of the States thereunder; and that I will in like manner abide by and faithfully support all Acts of Congress passed during the existing rebellion with reference to slaves, so long and so far as not repealed, modified or held void by Congress, or by decision of the Supreme Court; and that I will in like manner abide by and faithfully support all Proclamations of the President made during the existing rebellion, having reference to slaves, so long and so far as not modified or declared void by decision of the Supreme Court—So Help me God; and I give my solemn parole of honor (to be enforced according to military law,) that I will hold no correspondence with, or afford any aid or comfort to any enemies or opposers of the United States, save as an act of humanity, to administer to the necessities of individuals, who are in sickness or distress; and I solemnly declare that this Oath and Parole are taken and given freely and willingly, without any mental reservation or evasion whatever, and with full intention to keep the same.

Sworn and subscribed to, before me, th 22 day of May 1865.

George W Smith

[illegible]
Capt.
Provost Marshal.

Shortly after the Confederate surrender at Appomatox, Union provost marshals were dispatched throughout the South to require Southern men to sign an "oath and parole," giving their allegiance to the United States. George W. Smith of the Glebe signed this oath on May 22, 1865. (Courtesy of Betty Chowning.)

The *Richmond* is being loaded with lumber in Urbanna Creek. A lighter barge full of lumber is up against the side of the ram. Oakes Landing on Urbanna Creek was a regional landing where oxen, mules, and horses hauled wagonloads of wood from King and Queen, Gloucester, Essex, and Middlesex Counties. Most of the lumber was hauled either to Baltimore or Norfolk. (Courtesy of Buddy Davis.)

The two-masted schooner *Josephine* was a regular visitor to Urbanna. In this photograph, the vessel arrived in the creek during rainy weather. Note the crew left her sails up to dry in an effort to prevent the canvas from mildewing. Seen in the lower right, yachts were also regular visitors to the creek in the 1920s. (Courtesy of Emily Chowning.)

Owned by brothers Otho and Edward Smith of Urbanna, *Kate S. Tighlman* regularly moored on the creek. Some town schooner captains were J.H. Bohannon, E.S. Tomlinson, and William Gayle. (Courtesy of Buddy Davis.)

R. A. DAVIS

DEALER IN

SAWED LUMBER OF ALL KINDS

URBANNA, VA., 8–24–1921

Mast C.H. Palmer

1921 To R. A. Davis Dr.

To 4 Tons Coal @ 14.00 $56.00

Russell A. Davis operated a sawed-lumber business and owned several schooners. The *William Russell*, named after the owners Davis of Urbanna and William Segar of Stormont, was a frequent visitor to the creek. The schooner carried Davis and Segar's sawed lumber to Baltimore, but also was worked for hire. (Courtesy of Emily Chowning.)

The *David Carll*, later known as *Black Bird*, was one of the fastest schooners on the Chesapeake Bay. Owned by the Van Name family of New York, the boat was often seen on Urbanna Creek. (Courtesy of Dr. A.L. VanName.)

Usually, a sailing schooner or ram had a captain and mate aboard, and sometimes residents would pay them for passage to the city, instead of going by steamboat. Although steamboats carried a lot of small freight, bulk freight such as lumber, fertilizer, and other agricultural products were hauled in sailing vessels. When good roads and trucking advanced, the golden era of sail ended in Urbanna. (Courtesy of Dr. A.L. VanName.)

There were two creek landings on Urbanna Creek where lumber, grain, and other bulk freight was delivered and loaded onto sailing vessels and hauled to Baltimore. Oakes Landing was at the end of the road from Saluda, and Barn Landing was located on Rosegill property across from the town. (Courtesy of Dr. A.L. VanName.)

Large, three-masted rams occasionally frequented the landings on Urbanna Creek. When a large sailing ram came to the creek, it brought some excitement, as it was a bit unusual. (Courtesy of William C. Hight.)

Sailing yachts were also a part of the town fleet. The black-hulled *Nighthawk* used Urbanna Creek as its home port for many years. There were several sailing yachts on the creek in the 1930s and 1940s, when townsfolk lined the riverbanks to watch the annual races. Owned by H.V. Balwin, the *Nighthawk* was a favorite of the townspeople. Balwin was the owner of a major dry-goods store in Richmond, and was an active member of the Urbanna Sailing Association, founded in 1939. The vessel was conscripted in World War II, when it hunted down German submarine wolf packs off the Virginia Capes. (Courtesy of Roy Bowman and Dr. A.L. VanName.)

The *Quail* was a great competitor of the *Nighthawk*, and extremely competitive races between the two sailing yachts were held out in the Rappahannock River. The *Nighthawk* was the favorite of most townspeople because its captain Willie Buck lived in town. (Courtesy of Roy Bowman.)

Four

Steamboat Era

The golden era of steamboats began when two steam-powered, side-wheel vessels out of Norfolk named *Petersburg* and *Albemarle* arrived in 1821 at the mouth of the creek. In 1828, George Weems of Baltimore started the first commercial steamboat route on the Rappahannock River. The 123-foot *Patuxent* was used on the route. Main stops included Fredericksburg, Port Royal, Tappahannock, Carter's Creek, and Urbanna. In 1830, the Baltimore and Rappahannock Steam Packet Company started sending the steamboat *Rappahannock* to Urbanna. In 1845, Alfred Palmer opened Palmer's Wharf at the foot of Watling Street. The steamboat *Matilda* served the wharf then and was one of the first steamboats able to maneuver inside the creek.

Steamboat traffic increased as propeller and screw-driven boats arrived. These vessels were able to enter and turn around in the creek with relative ease. Columbus Burton purchased Palmer's Wharf in the 1880s, John Gressitt opened Gressitt's Wharf where the Urbanna Town Marina is located today, and Donaldson's Wharf was located in front of what is Queen Anne's Cove Condominiums today. Along the river, West Urbanna Wharf was constructed in 1871 by the Baltimore and Susquehanna Steam Company.

Modern trucks and good roads for automobiles slowed the use of steamboats and the "August Storm" hurricane of 1933 destroyed many of the wharfs. The last steamboat to enter Urbanna Creek was in 1937, when the *Anne Arundel* came down from Baltimore on a final trip. On the day she came and went, people closed their businesses and came out of their homes to watch the end of an era.

Steamboats frequented the three Urbanna landings on the creek and the river. (Courtesy of *Southside Sentinel.*)

The arrival of a steamboat on Mondays brought townsfolk down to meet the boat. The steamboat provided access to city conveniences. In the 1920s, a husband's Sunday shirt could be loaded on the steamboat, delivered to a Chinese laundry in Baltimore, and arrive, pressed and clean, before the next Sunday church gathering. (Courtesy of *Southside Sentinel.*)

Urbanna board of trade members petitioned the steamboat company and Virginia General Assembly to have Burton's Wharf changed to Urbanna Wharf–No. 12 and have West Urbanna Wharf changed to Remlik Wharf. When a Works Progress Administration (WPA) photographer captured this image in 1937, the name had changed to Urbanna Wharf–No. 12. (Courtesy of Library of Virginia.)

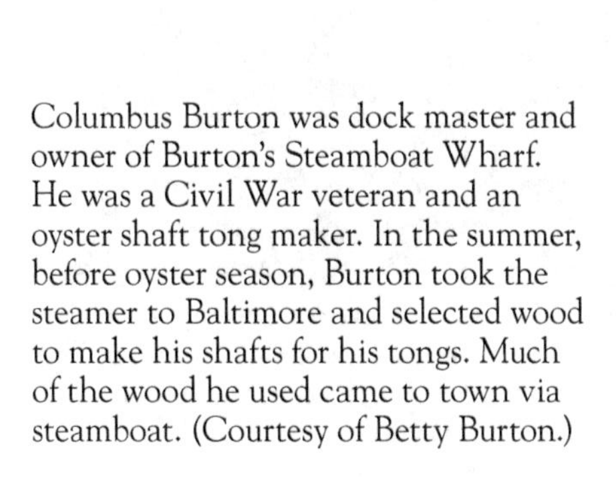

Columbus Burton was dock master and owner of Burton's Steamboat Wharf. He was a Civil War veteran and an oyster shaft tong maker. In the summer, before oyster season, Burton took the steamer to Baltimore and selected wood to make his shafts for his tongs. Much of the wood he used came to town via steamboat. (Courtesy of Betty Burton.)

A trail of smoke and steam whistles alerted the town that a steamboat was arriving. (Courtesy of the Middlesex County Public Library.)

This stevedore stands in the side-hold hatch of a steamboat in Urbanna. Stevedores were responsible for loading cattle, chickens, eggs, vegetables, furs, and other items bound for the city market. The steamboat also brought city goods back to town. The first automobile arrived in town in 1911 at Burton's Wharf in the hold of a steamboat. (Courtesy of Betty Burton.)

Although Urbanna Creek was one of the widest and deepest creeks on the Rappahannock River, it was years before steamboats regularly served landings inside the creek. On August 14, 1882, the steamer *Mason L. Weems* ran hard aground in the creek, and the vessel had to be off-loaded of all its goods. A week later, she was freed on an extreme high tide. (Courtesy of Middlesex County Public Library.)

Two steamboats moored together on Urbanna Creek was a sight seldom seen. On occasion, the anticipation of a bad storm brought steamboats into the creek for safe haven. (Courtesy of Betty Burton.)

West Urbanna Wharf, also called Nelson Wharf, and later, Remlik Wharf, was a favorite vacation spot for many from Baltimore and Washington who came to relax at Captain Lang Nelson's Hotel near the wharf. Urbanna's mail was delivered to West Urbanna Wharf via steamboat; before automobiles, the town postmaster rode his horse to the wharf daily to pick up the mail. (Courtesy of Town of Urbanna.)

Hotel Nelson was located in front of Remlik Wharf. In this post-1909 postcard, the wharf's name has changed from West Urbanna to Remlik Wharf. Hotel Nelson was run and operated by Capt. Lang Nelson. The steamboat brought vacationers from Baltimore and Norfolk regularly and Captain Lang ran a booming business until the steamboat era ended. (Courtesy of Emily Chowning.)

In the 1920s, steamboats *Talbot* and *Potomac* were favorite vessels of those living in town. These propeller-driven boats, unlike side-wheelers, were able to maneuver inside the creek and land at the town docks. (Courtesy of Buddy Davis.)

This steamboat is passing Gressitt's Dock on its way out of Urbanna Creek. The three-log canoe oyster boat in the foreground is powered by a small engine near the stern. During oyster season, there were so many boats like this on the creek that when they all cranked up early in the morning it sounded like a melody of putts and knocks. (Courtesy of Betty Burton.)

Pictured here, state police boat *Accomac* is approaching West Urbanna Steamboat Wharf. When steamboats were not there, Urbanna wharfs were busy with local commerce, and state and private vessels often landed. (Courtesy of *Southside Sentinel.*)

A steamboat arrival was an exciting event for the people in town. When the era ended, many longed for the steamboat whistle, the good food served in the dining hall, and a gentle night's sleep in an upper berth of a stateroom. (Courtesy of William C. Hight.)

Five

Business and Waterfront

The business community has been a vibrant part of town life since its start. Commerce grew from the waterfront as the tobacco trade generated warehouses, a customhouse, Scottish factor stores, and other types of Colonial commerce. The steamboat encouraged commercial activity near the wharfs.

The oyster, fish, crab, and vegetable canning businesses brought seafood processing houses, canneries, and pickle factories. An ice plant, a flourmill, granary, broom factory, tannery, blacksmith, and an overall and shirt factory were a part of the town's commerce. The weekly newspaper *Southside Sentinel* was founded in 1896, and the first bank in town, the Bank of Middlesex, opened in 1900.

A silent movie theater, several automobile dealerships, and Coca-Cola Bottling Works (with "Urbanna" embossed on the bottom of the bottles) opened in the 1920s. In the 1930s and 1940s, Riva Rink roller-skating and bowling alley and Rappanna (movie) Theater, brought people to town on Saturday nights from near and far. In the 1950s, Southside Marine grew into one of the largest railway/marinas in the state.

In 1958, Marshall's Drug Store served reasonably priced lunches. The drugstore served a 15¢ tomato and lettuce sandwich, a 5¢ small coke, and a 5¢ bag of potato chips. The Urbanna Beach Hotel and Hurley's Hotel brought visitors to town year after year in the 1950s. Renowned chef Joe Cameron cooked at Christchurch School during the school year and served some of the best fried soft-shell crabs in the world for guests of Urbanna Beach Hotel in the summer. The creek and river have lured vacationers, anglers, crabbers, and oystermen to town for years, and commerce has relied heavily on the advantages created by Urbanna Creek and Rappahannock River.

Ross House Hotel on Watling Street catered to visitors arriving by steamboat and folks traveling from West Point by train. The hotel had horse-drawn carriages that went to West Point to pick up drummers, visitors, and supplies arriving there by train. (Courtesy of Middlesex County Public Library.)

Jonathan and Edmonia Ross founded the Ross House Hotel and built what is today Haywood's Store on Walting Street around 1875. John and Edmonia were known as giving people. They gave land for Urbanna Baptist Church and donated the use of a home on Prince George Street to aged widows unable to support themselves. (Courtesy of Emily Chowning.)

The back portion of the Ross House had gardens, a pavilion, and a boathouse for the launch *Gentry*. (Courtesy of Emily Chowning.)

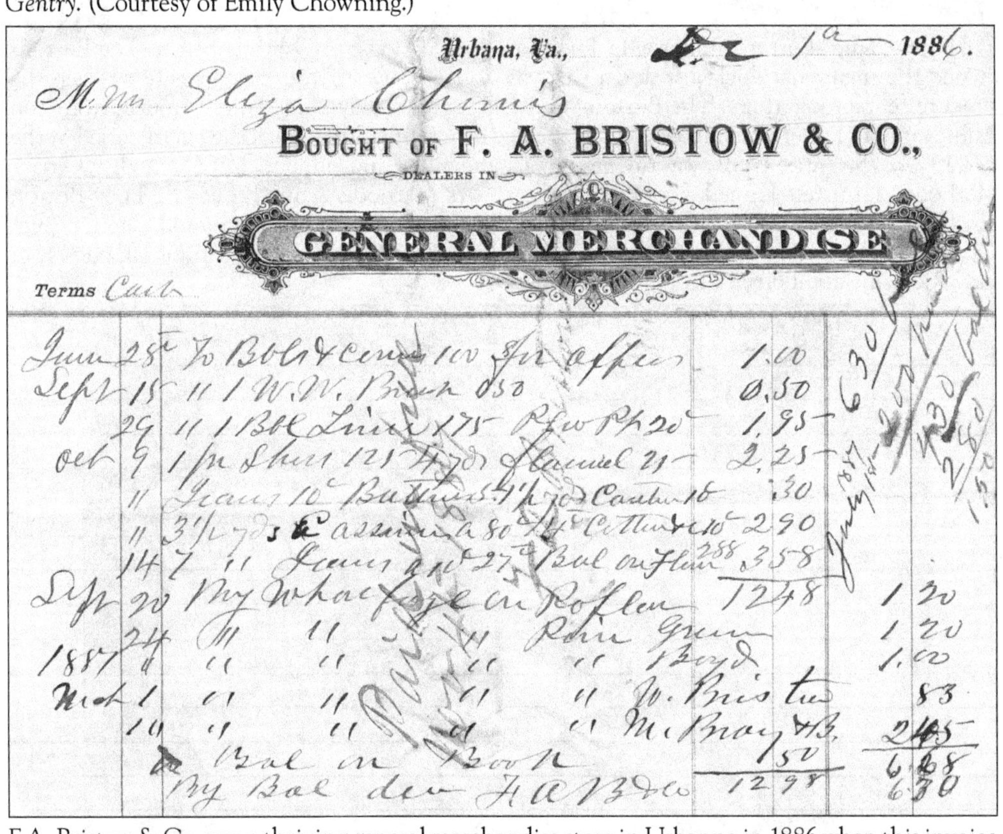

Urbana, Va., 1886.

BOUGHT OF F. A. BRISTOW & CO.,

DEALERS IN

GENERAL MERCHANDISE

Terms

F.A. Bristow & Co. was a thriving general merchandise store in Urbanna in 1886 when this invoice for Eliza Chowning was drafted. Bristow founded his general store in 1869. His main competitor was B.E. Cornwell & Son on Virginia Street, which once stood opposite the present post office. (Courtesy of Betty Chowning.)

Columbus "Lum" Burton and his wife, Lucy, ran Burton House on Watling Street. The Burtons owned the steamboat dock just down the way, so that new arrivals could easily walk up the street to rent a room there. The Burton family (below) was a dynamic family unit. Burton's son Aubrey ran his father's steamboat dock at the end of Watling Street until the wharf closed in the late 1930s. The entire family was talented in art and music and emphatically Methodist. Circuit Methodist ministers longed to preach at the town's Methodist church because Lucy Burton served up a wonderful Tidewater Virginia home-cooked meal after church, and Captain Lum slipped the minister $6 for their efforts, good or bad, in payment for their sermon. (Courtesy of Judy Richwine and Betty Burton.)

Columbus Burton wrote in his 1898 logbook that he made and repaired 105 wooden oyster tong shafts. He made sculling oars, crab-net handles, and bailing scoops. He also purchased one old log canoe a year, like the one pictured here, for about $25 and sold it for $75 after repairs. (Author's collection.)

Gaslights are visible outside R.S. Bristow's store at the intersection of Virginia and Cross Streets. R.S. Bristow & Son, "Home of Good Goods," was established in 1876; this store was built in 1898. Gas streetlights were used until 1912, when the first electric streetlights were installed. (Courtesy of Beth Maxwell.)

The Bank of Middlesex received its charter in December 1900. William C. Nalle of Irvington, and Fredericksburg residents A. Randolph Howard, William Augustine Smith, Edgar M. Young Jr., and F. Lightfoot Howard were the first directors. Judge of the Middlesex County Circuit T.R.B. Wright granted the charter. The bank building was completed in 1902. (Courtesy of Middlesex County Public Library.)

The Urbanna Manufacturing Co., including an excelsior plant and an overalls and shirt factory, opened in 1901 and closed around 1915. After closing, the building was eventually converted into Urbanna Beach Hotel. The hotel was a vacation spot for visitors coming from Richmond and elsewhere. It was torn down in the 1980s to make way for the construction of the Queen Anne's Cove Condominiums. (Courtesy of Middlesex County Public Library.)

The Urbanna Manufacturing Co. was founded by Fredericksburg businessman A. Randolph Howard. Branch Standard Overall Factory was a division of the company, employing over 30 women. A week's wages ranged from $3 to $7. The c. 1905 photograph above shows workers at the plant. Howard also spearheaded the incorporation of the town, which the state legislature approved on April 2, 1902. In 1908, another division of the company manufactured excelsior, a woodchip used in packaging, cushioning, and stuffing. The excelsior plant was located down on the water in front of the shirt factory, and product was shipped on sailing schooners from Donaldson's Wharf to Baltimore and Norfolk markets. (Courtesy of L.M. and Albert Carlton and Middlesex County Public Library.)

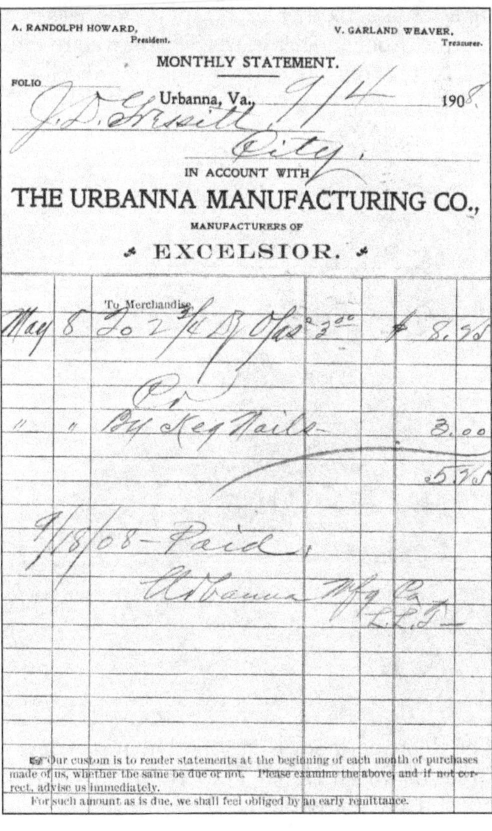

A. RANDOLPH HOWARD, President.
V. GARLAND WEAVER, Treasurer.

MONTHLY STATEMENT.

FOLIO

Urbanna, Va., 190

IN ACCOUNT WITH

THE URBANNA MANUFACTURING CO.,

MANUFACTURERS OF

EXCELSIOR.

To Merchandise,

Our custom is to render statements at the beginning of each month of purchases made of us, whether the same be due or not. Please examine the above, and if not correct, advise us immediately.

For such amount as is due, we shall feel obliged by an early remittance.

Along with the Urbanna Manufacturing Co., the firm built a row of two-story houses to accommodate supervisors and other important personnel associated with the business. When the factory closed, refugees from Tangier Island, who moved to Urbanna after the "August Storm," purchased homes on "cottage row." (Courtesy of Joe Cardwell.)

The Rappahannock River and Urbanna Creek waterfront was a drawing card for city visitors to Urbanna Beach Hotel. They enjoyed the salt-water atmosphere that came with staying at the hotel. (Courtesy of Emily Chowning.)

Rosegill Shore was on the east side of Urbanna Creek. In the early years, Urbanna Beach Hotel rented skiffs that customers rowed across to Rosegill Beach, where they could swim, fish, crab, and search for shells, arrowheads, and shark teeth. (Courtesy of the Middlesex County Public Library.)

C.A. Taylor operated a grocery store on the corner leading into the overall and shirt factory building. Judging from this 1907 invoice, his Urbanna Meat Market sold more than just "chops and steaks." Celery, apples, oranges, cabbage, pineapples, nuts, and lima beans were part of Taylor's inventory. (Courtesy of Middlesex County Public Library.)

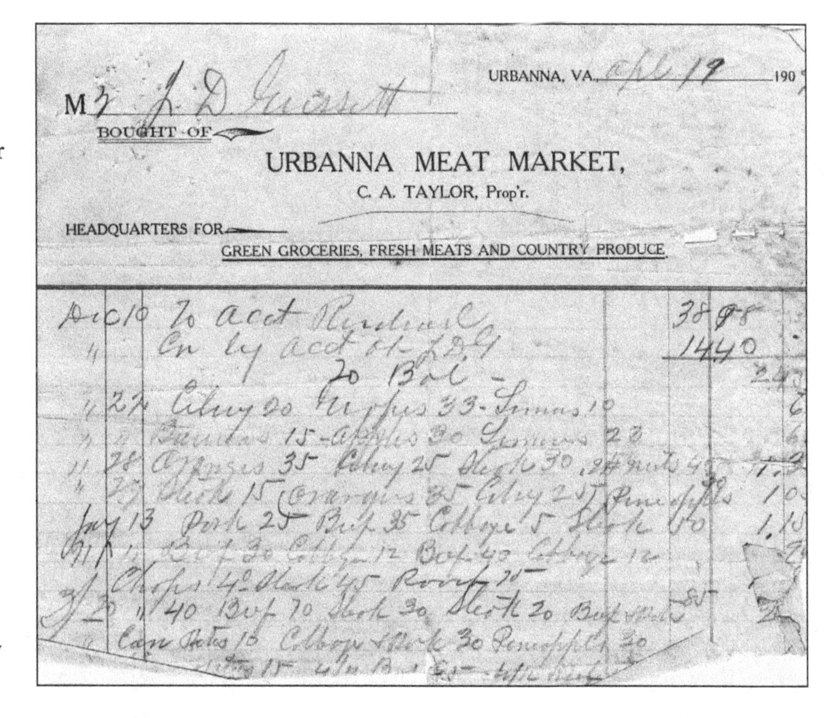
URBANNA, VA., Apl 19 190

M J. D. Garrett

BOUGHT OF

URBANNA MEAT MARKET,

C. A. TAYLOR, Prop'r.

HEADQUARTERS FOR

GREEN GROCERIES, FRESH MEATS AND COUNTRY PRODUCE.

Pickle factories, Powell's Mill ice plant, and J.W. Hurley's Oyster House are pictured in this 1920s waterfront photograph. Numsen Manufacturing Co., Standard Pickling Co., Donaldson & Shultz Co., C.A. Hotchkiss, J.W. Hurley, and Max and Harry Borton all operated pickle factories in or near town limits. (Courtesy of *Southside Sentinel.*)

R.A. Davis, J.W. Hurley, and Kriente owned canning factories along the creek shore, some going back to 1870. The factories canned tomatoes, potatoes, huckleberries, and blackberries. J.W. Hurley used an image of his son Boyd on his Urbanna Brand Tomato label. (Courtesy of Emily Chowning.)

Urbanna also had blacksmith and farrier shops. Wheeley & Pierce were general blacksmiths and wheelwrights in 1910. According to this invoice, Charles Wheeley and Joe Pierce shoed horses, installed new tires on buggies, repaired buggy shafts, and fixed wheel spokes and rims. (Courtesy of Middlesex County Public Library.)

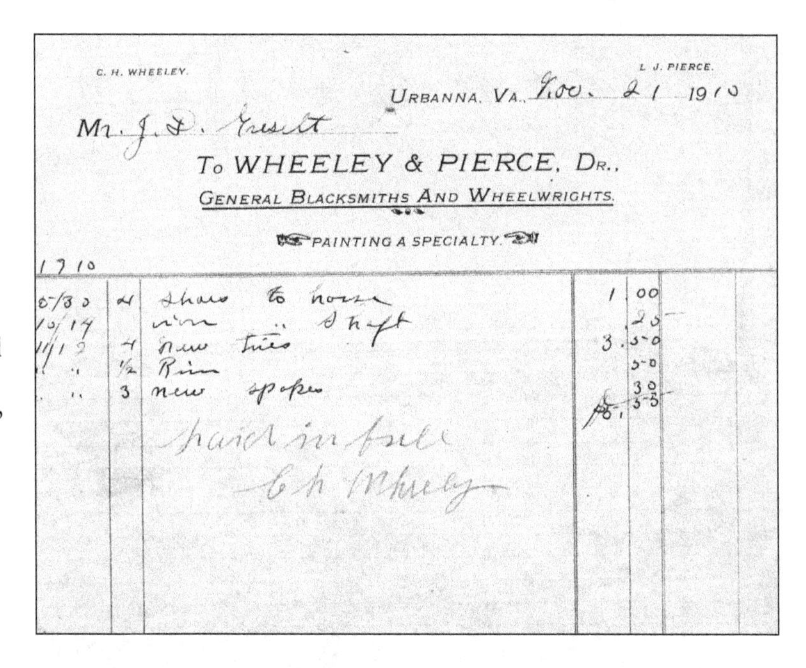

C. H. WHEELEY. L. J. PIERCE.

URBANNA, VA., Nov. 21 1910

Mr. J. D. Gressitt

To WHEELEY & PIERCE, DR.,

GENERAL BLACKSMITHS AND WHEELWRIGHTS.

PAINTING A SPECIALTY.

1910

8/30	4	shoes to horse	1.00
10/19		iron " shaft	.25
11/12	4	new tires	3.50
"	1/2	Rim	.50
"	3	new spokes	.30
			$5.55

Paid in full
C H Wheeley

P. N. RILEE L. J. PIERCE

To RILEE & PIERCE, Dr.

GENERAL BLACKSMITHS AND WHEELWRIGHTS

Horse-Shoeing a Specialty

Urbanna, Va., Nov. 4 1912

Mr. J. D. Gressitt

1912

April 20	1	brace for monkey rail	.60
May 9		repairs on chain	.40
" 31		boat work	.35
July 22	4	shoes to horse	1.00
Sept. 31		repairs on block	.10
" "	1	bolt	.05
			$2.40
			80
			160

By 1912, the blacksmith shop had become Rilee & Pierce and was doing more work on oyster boats than shoeing horses, as revealed by this invoice to J.D. Gressitt. Gressitt had four new shoes put on his horse for $1, but the rest of his invoice reflected work on his boat. (Courtesy of Middlesex County Public Library.)

Town businessmen often utilized deckboats, like *Secret*, to haul merchandise purchased from wholesale stores in Norfolk and Baltimore back to town. Some merchants owned their own boats while others hired a boat, captain, and crew to pick up and deliver their goods. (Courtesy of Sam Richardson.)

By the time of this photograph, Gressitt's Wharf had changed to the Standard Oil Dock. Note that fuel tanks can be seen in the distance. Large fuel boats arrived weekly to keep up with the demand for gasoline. Urbanna's general merchandise stores were the first gas stations in town, with hand-operated pumps. Hurley's seafood is in the foreground. (Courtesy of Betty Chowning.)

This 1911 photograph shows the L.L. Tignor Co. Department Store (haberdashers) and Jones & Chowning drug store on Virginia Street. The first automobile in town arrived around 1910, reportedly a red Cadillac that belonged to Sen. J. Henry Cochran of Rosegill. (Courtesy of *Southside Sentinel.*)

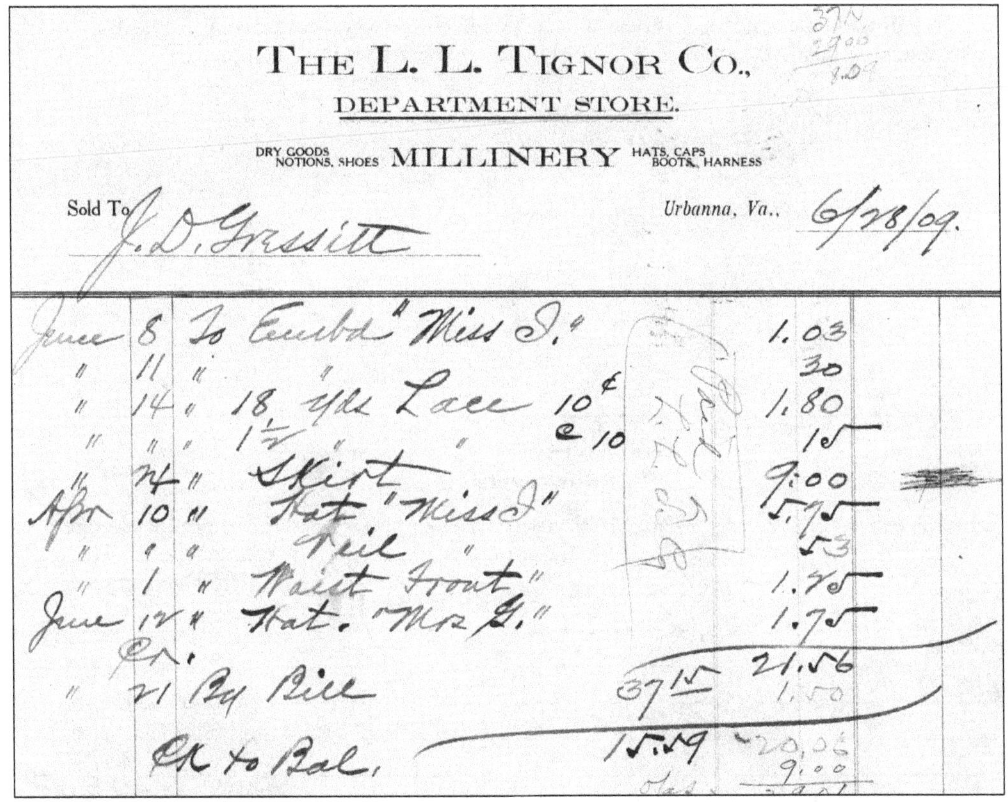

THE L. L. TIGNOR CO.,
DEPARTMENT STORE.

DRY GOODS NOTIONS, SHOES MILLINERY HATS, CAPS BOOTS, HARNESS

Sold To J. D. Gressitt

Urbanna, Va., 6/28/09.

June	8	To Embd "Miss I."		1.03
"	11	"		30
"	14	" 18 yds Lace	10¢	1.80
"	"	" 1½ " "	@ 10	15
"	24	" Skirt		9.00
Apr	10	" Hat "Miss I"		5.75
"	"	" Veil "		53
"	1	" Waist Front "		1.25
June	12	" Hat. "Mrs G."		1.75
		Cr.		21.56
"	21	By Bill	37.15	1.50
		Cr to Bal.	15.59	20.06
				9.00

This invoice from June 28, 1909, states that Mrs. J.D. Gressitt paid 10¢ a yard for lace, $9 for a skirt, $1.25 for a waist front, $1.75 for a hat, and $5.75 for a fine hat at the L.L. Tignor Co. Department Store. The invoice also states that Tignor's sold dry goods, notions, shoes, hats, caps, boots, and harness. (Courtesy of Middlesex County Public Library.)

Urbanna's waterfront was busy in the 1920s. Southside Marine, the large building over the water, was a repair and boatbuilding business that helped keep the town's oyster fleet operating. In just a few years, the business would cater to yachts. (Courtesy of *Southside Sentinel*.)

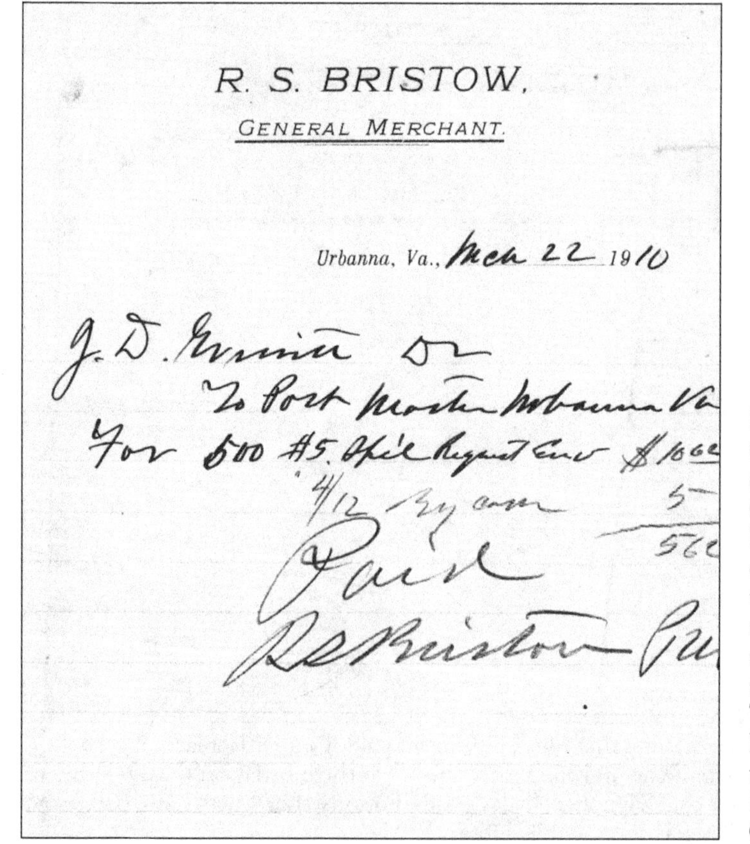

R. S. BRISTOW,

GENERAL MERCHANT.

Urbanna, Va., Mch 22 1910

J. D. [illegible] Dr

To Post Master Urbanna Va

For 500 #5. Offi'l Request Env $10.60

4/12 By [illegible] 5—

5.60

Paid

R S Bristow Pm

In 1775, the Second Continental Congress created the US Post Office Department. Urbanna had a post office in 1776. The town was described in 1823 as a "post village and a seaport town with a population of 175." This invoice states that Robert S. Bristow Sr. was postmaster in 1910. (Courtesy of Middlesex County Public Library.)

This 1920s aerial photograph shows bustling waterfront commerce fueled by the comings and goings of commercial sailing schooners and other waterborne commerce. The schooners hauled freight and other goods in and out of town. The introduction of good roads and trucks in the 1940s eliminated the need for sailing schooners. (Courtesy of Emily Chowning.)

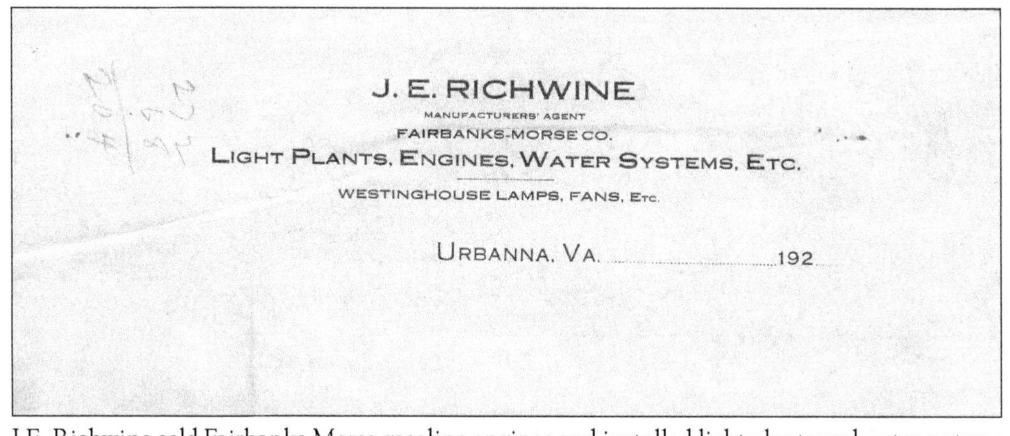

J. E. RICHWINE

MANUFACTURERS' AGENT

FAIRBANKS-MORSE CO.

LIGHT PLANTS, ENGINES, WATER SYSTEMS, ETC.

WESTINGHOUSE LAMPS, FANS, ETC.

URBANNA, VA. 192

J.E. Richwine sold Fairbanks-Morse gasoline engines and installed light plants and water systems in the 1920s. He opened the first silent movie theater at Regal Building, built around 1914. The Regal Building is now Urbanna Town Hall. (Courtesy of Emily Chowning.)

Richardson's Drug Store was the main drug store before Dr. Thomas F. Marshall bought Richardson's out and opened Marshall's Drug Store. In this early 1920s postcard, Richardson's is next to the bank building, and Harper's General Store is father down on the corner of Prince George and Bank (later Cross) Streets. (Courtesy of Kevin Barrick.)

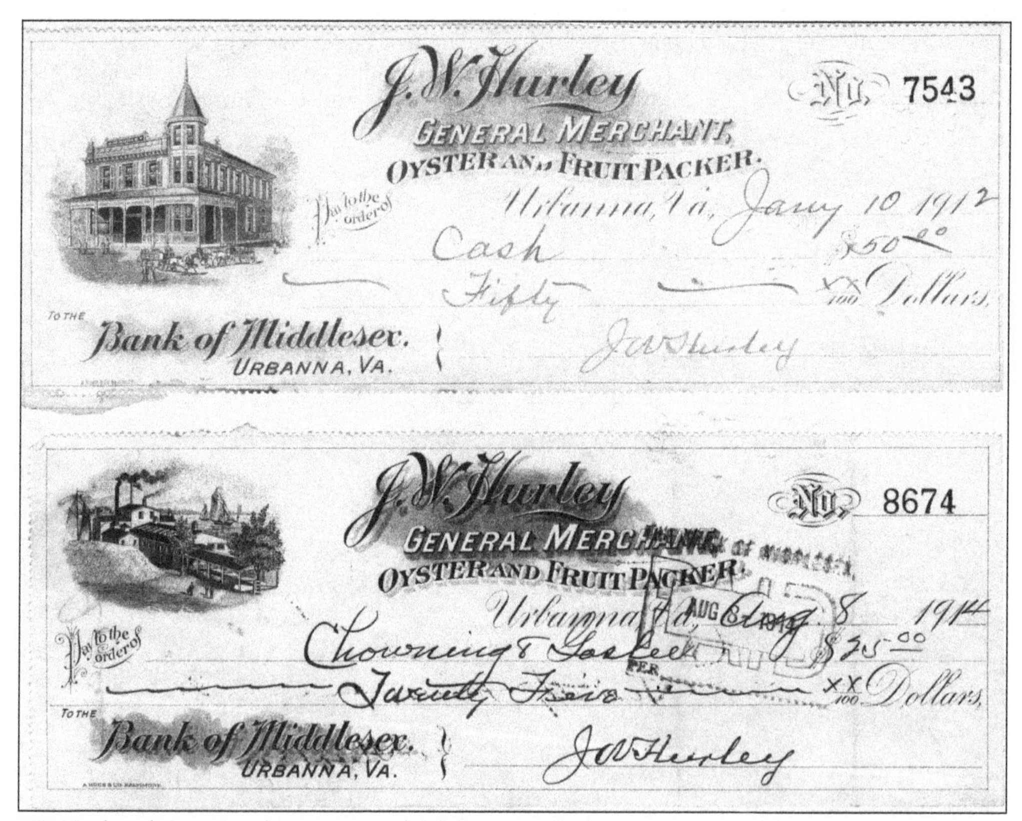

J. W. Hurley
GENERAL MERCHANT,
OYSTER AND FRUIT PACKER.
No. 7543
Urbanna, Va, Jany 10 1912
Pay to the order of Cash $50.00
Fifty xx/100 Dollars,
To the Bank of Middlesex. URBANNA, VA.
J W Hurley

J. W. Hurley
GENERAL MERCHANT,
OYSTER AND FRUIT PACKER.
No. 8674
Urbanna Va, Aug 8 1914
Pay to the order of Chowning & Gaskell $25.00
Twenty Five xx/100 Dollars,
To the Bank of Middlesex. URBANNA, VA.
J W Hurley

J.W. Hurley also operated an oyster and fish house and a tomato-canning factory. The firm located at the foot of Virginia Street was in full swing when these checks were issued in 1912 and 1914. (Courtesy of Selden Richardson.)

During the 1940s, large schools of croakers came into the Rappahannock, and some fishermen made small fortunes by harvesting the fish in haul seine nets. These men are sorting fish at J.W. Hurley & Son after a big catch. (Courtesy of Grace Daniel.)

J. W. HURLEY & SON

DEALERS IN

FISH, HARD AND SOFT CRABS

Urbanna, Va., ..., 195....

Bought Of

____

....	lbs. Small Rock	@	lb.	$
....	lbs. Medium Rock	@	lb	$
....	lbs. Large Rock	@	lb.	$
....	lbs. Croakers	@	lb.	$
....	lbs. No. 1 Spot	@	lb.	$
....	lbs. No. 2 Spot	@	lb.	$
....	lbs. Medium Blues	@	lb.	$
....	lbs. Large Blues	@	lb.	$
....	lbs. Buck Shad	@	lb.	$
....	lbs. Roe Shad	@	lb.	$
....	lbs. Jacks	@	lb.	$
....	lbs. Herring	@	lb.	$
....	lbs. Large Grays	@	lb.	$
....	lbs. Medium Grays	@	lb.	$
....	lbs. Pan Grays	@	lb.	$
....	lbs. Salmon Trout	@	lb.	$
....	lbs. Flounders	@	lb.	$
....	lbs. Cats	@	lb.	$
....	lbs. Carp	@	lb.	$
....	lbs.	@	lb.	$

J W. HURLEY & SON

By ______________________

J.W. Hurley & Son dealt in all types of locally caught fish and crabs, as this invoice reveals. The seafood firm was one of the largest in the region and provided fresh fish, crabs, and oysters to its customers. (Courtesy of Walt Hurley.)

Oyster buy boat *Gracie Lee* (the boat with the house to the rear) was owned by Alvin Daniel. The above photograph shows how oyster tong boats rafted up to an oyster buy boat in Rappahannock River so oysters could be hoisted from smaller boats into the hold of the *Gracie Lee*. The buy boat then took oysters to an oyster-processing house. At left, Ben Wormeley unloads oysters from the buy boat *Grace*. The metal tub full of oysters is referred to as a "Virginia measure," which is a little more than a bushel of oysters. (Courtesy of Grace Daniel and Jonesey Payne.)

URBANNA, VA. March 9 1900

Mr R H Woodward

BOUGHT OF JNO. D. GRESSITT,

DEALER IN

GENERAL MERCHANDISE.

1900 PLANTER AND SHIPPER OF SHELL OYSTERS. AGENT FOR STANDARD OIL CO.

March 9	4 Ton Guano Freight	4 00		
	Whf 40 Putting Guano in house	56	4 56	
	By All Bill	90		
	" Cash	3 66		

Paid J D Gressitt

Jonathan D. Gressitt was a general merchandise storekeeper in Urbanna who was "a planter and shipper of shell oysters" and a Standard Oil supplier. When oysters were plentiful, the oyster business drove the town economy and most everyone was involved in some manner. (Courtesy of Bettie James.)

Boyd Hurley stands in his father's oyster-shucking house in the late 1800s. The oyster business was an important part of the local economy from the 1820s to 1960s, when a newly introduced oyster disease called MSX began killing oysters all over Chesapeake Bay and the oyster business declined. The oyster house was torn down in 1988. (Courtesy of Jonesey Payne.)

Inside the oyster house, shuckers stand in their stalls and shuck oysters. The men were paid piecemeal for the amount of oysters they shucked. The faster they shucked the more money they earned. Oyster shuckers worked long hours at Hurley's oyster house. Shucking oysters was laborious work, and during the day, shuckers often broke out in song to pass the time. When children were out of school, they would sometimes wander down to the shucking house, sit outside the door, and listen to the men sing spirituals, some left over from the time of slavery. (Courtesy of Jonesey Payne.)

Once shucked, the raw product was sealed in Hurley's oyster cans and shipped to customers up and down the East Coast. Hurley cans are rare today and bring a good price from collectors of old oyster cans. (Courtesy of Jonesey Payne.)

Baby oysters or "spat" were delivered to Urbanna on buy boats. The boats went to James River where the seed oysters were bought from men harvesting spat using hand tongs. After loading, oysters were hauled to Urbanna and planted on privately leased oyster beds in the Rappahannock River and Urbanna Creek. (Author's collection.)

The *Nellie Crockett*, an oyster buy boat, moored on the creek the night before the load of seed was planted. Once a common sight on Urbanna Creek, this photograph taken in 1985 shows the last traditional oyster buy boat loaded with seed oysters to enter the creek, ending a long, cultural era for the town. The commercial oyster farming business on Rappahannock River goes back to the early 1800s. (Author's collection.)

Lord Mott Corporation operated a vegetable-canning factory on what had been the West Urbanna Steamboat Wharf. Lord Mott Canning Factory became one of the largest vegetable packing plants along the East Coast, and was a major employer of Urbanna men and women from 1934 to the late 1970s. (Courtesy of *Southside Sentinel*.)

The "Big" *Muriel Eileen*, built in 1928, was a buy boat used to haul freight and oysters. She was called the "Big" *Muriel Eileen* because her owner R.E. Roberts of Lord Mott Corporation already had a smaller vessel named the *Muriel Eileen*, built in 1926. Both vessels were named for his two daughters, Muriel and Eileen. The "Big" *Muriel Eileen* sank in 1969 in the Atlantic Ocean, while working in the clam-dredging fishery. Today, Owner David Cantera and his family from New Castle, Delaware, have converted "Little" *Muriel Eileen* into a yacht. The vessel occasionally visits Urbanna in the summer. (Courtesy of George Mills.)

Once a year for a vacation on the Chesapeake Bay, R.E. Roberts brought his family down from Baltimore to cruise on the "Big" *Muriel Eileen*. The canvas awning was only used when the boat was being used for pleasure. The rest of the year, the boat was used to haul produce, cans, and supplies between Urbanna and Baltimore. (Courtesy of William C. Hight.)

Muriel and Eileen Roberts pose on a couple of mules with their father, R.E. Roberts, owner of Lord Mott Corp. in Baltimore, the Lord Mott Canning Factory, and Morattico Packing Company in Urbanna. (Courtesy of David Cantera.)

The Original Floating Theater visited Urbanna in the summer starting in 1914 and ending about 1941. Inside a 128-foot by 34-foot barge, the theater was towed by two tugboats and moored at the end of Virginia Street. The novelty brought people to town from all over the region. Plays were performed on a 19-foot stage by a professional troupe from New York. (Courtesy of Virginia Burton.)

The "Big" *Muriel Eileen* and *John Branford* are docked at Southern States Granary at the foot of Virginia Street in the 1950s. Wooden boats hauled corn, wheat, and soybeans from Urbanna to Norfolk. The grain elevators were torn down in the early 2000s, and a hotel was built on the site. (Courtesy of William C. Hight.)

Well into the 1990s, large steel-hulled "bay boats" loaded wheat, corn, and soybeans at Southern States Granary and hauled it to Norfolk. During harvest season, town streets provided amble food for songbirds as wind blew a little grain here and there off trucks bound for the granary. In the 1960s, Urbanna was made an official songbird sanctuary. (Courtesy of William C. Hight.)

A grain boat is loaded with corn at the granary. J.W. Hurley & Son Seafood, later called Payne's Crab House, can be seen in the background. The seafood house was torn down in 1988. (Courtesy of *Southside Sentinel.*)

Beginning on May 15, 1924, private ferry *Frances B. Garrett* ran three days a week across the Rappahannock between Irvington and Urbanna. Ferries ran across the river until the Robert O. Norris (Rappahannock River) Bridge opened on August 30, 1957. (Courtesy of Middlesex County Public Library.)

When the mouth of Urbanna Creek was dredged in the early 1920s, the spoils were used to create a long jut of land with a rock jetty extending out into the river to keep the mouth of the creek from silting in. Houses were later built on the jut of land; this postcard shows the first house built on what was called Broad Shore. (Courtesy of Middlesex County Public Library.)

The northern border of the town runs along the Rappahannock River. This 1958 aerial photograph shows Broad Shore on the Rappahannock River and undeveloped areas of town. There were still fields throughout town where vegetables were grown. All the fields are now gone, as houses have been built where tomatoes, string beans, and peas once grew. Today, the Urbanna United Methodist Church is located where, in 1958, pickers worked the fields to provide product for Lord Mott Canning Factory. During picking season, residents lowered their windows to hear the sweet songs of the African American women pickers. "Honestly, I've never heard a church choir that sounded any better," recalled one resident. (Courtesy of *Southside Sentinel*.)

Hurley's Restaurant was booming in the 1940s. Once, Dr. A.L. VanName brought guests to Hurley's when there was a long line at the door. VanName received a call that a patient was having a baby, which he then delivered, arriving back at the restaurant only to see his wife and guest just getting through the entrance. (Courtesy of Kevin Barrick.)

Central water came to Urbanna in 1910. Prior to that time, brick-lined wells some 40 feet deep were dug for each household. The water tower was torn down in the 1960s when the town moved its well and treatment plant outside of town. This 1930s photograph shows the water tower at right. (Courtesy of Betty Burton.)

For many years, the town had its own broom factory down on the waterfront, but mops and brooms out of cornhusks and hickory were made at home. Every country store in town had a barrel full of these mops, particularly for oystermen to clean their boats. The mops generally sold for whatever a bushel of oysters was bringing that day, perhaps 25¢. (Author's collection.)

During the 1940s and 1950s, the post office was located in the downstairs of the 1902 bank building. The side door next to the post office led to a stairway to Dr. Stanley Hart's dentist office in the upstairs of the bank building. Marshall's Drug Store was next door. (Courtesy of Middlesex County Public Library.)

The Texaco Automobile Service Station, operated by Max Hibble, was in the center of town in the 1950s. In the background, Bonner's Store once housed the Silver Slipper, a barroom business. (Courtesy of Richard Marshall.)

Dr. Thomas F. Marshall Sr. built the first ABC store and leased it to the state in the 1940s. The store had just been built on Virginia Street when this photograph was taken. Across the river, Lancaster County was a dry county. On Saturdays, the Tides Inn of Irvington ran a passenger cruise to Urbanna on the yacht *Miss Ann* called the "whiskey run." (Courtesy of Richard Marshall.)

Bonners at the corner of Virginia and Cross Streets served candies, cold sodas, and ice cream as the store awning advertised. Note that "City Bus" was meant to be a humorous inscription. (Courtesy of the *Southside Sentinel*.)

The River Rink, a skating rink and bowling alley, was the main entertainment center of the town until 1947, when it burned. For years thereafter, many local married couples pinpointed the moment "the love bug bit" when they were skating arm-in-arm at the River Rink. (Courtesy of Bob Henkel.)

In this 1942 photograph, a couple poses on the deck that surrounds the River Rink. Urbanna men fought in every war from the Revolutionary War to the Vietnam War. Howard Street is named in honor of Howard Bristow, killed in World War II. (Courtesy of J.D. Davis.)

The excitement and joy of youth can be sensed from this photograph of a young gal sitting on the rail of the River Rink over Urbanna Creek in 1942. The horrors and fears of World War II did not dampen the gentle smiles and beautiful, unblemished faces of youth. (Courtesy of J.D. Davis.)

The Hurley Hotel and restaurant can be seen here on the right, and J.W. Hurley & Son Seafood is on the left. High water sometimes hampered business down on the waterfront. (Courtesy of Richard Marshall.)

The 5¢ 10¢ to $1 Store, on the corner of Virginia and Cross Streets, was owned by Elliot Richardson and his wife. The store featured a variety of goods, and was a major retail store in town until it closed in the 1980s. (Courtesy of Elizabeth Richardson.)

The only Urbanna store owned by an African American in the 1950s was located next to where the wooden bridge once ended at the foot of Watling Street. Wash Thornton ran a general merchandise store and operated a barbershop in the back room. Before the wooden bridge was torn down, Thornton operated the draw and was the town bridge keeper. (Courtesy of Joe Conboy.)

CHEVROLET
CARS AND ACCESSORIES

SMITH BROS.

STANDARD OIL CO.'S PRODUCTS
CHEVROLET AND FORD AUTO REPAIRS
LUBRICATING AND MACHINE OILS
CHICKEN GRIT

Garage, Gasoline and Coal Oil Station

House and Auto Paints. Standard-make Auto Tires and Tubes

URBANNA, VA., Mar 2 1920

Sold to

We Smith Bros. have sold and delivered to Chas Palmer one Four ninety Chevrolet Touring Car no 189714. in which Chas Palmer has paid $400.00 four hundred cash. and give his notes for $350.00 three fifty to be paid one hundred every two months until paid for this 2 day of March 1920.

(Signed) Smith Bros.
Per R Otho Smith

Moter No C96087

Over the years, there have been numerous automobile dealerships in Urbanna. Smith Bros. sold Chevrolets in 1920. They ran a garage, sold gasoline, and delivered coal to townsfolk. Coal was the main fuel used for heat, while wood was used for cook stoves. (Courtesy of Emily Chowning.)

This 1920s housewife shows off her new, wooden Juno cook stove at her home in town. A brand new cook stove was a source of pride in those days. Many homes in Urbanna did not have electricity until after the 1930s. Even then, some continued to use wood cook stoves. Food just tasted better, some thought. (Courtesy of L.M. and Albert Carlton.)

Cars parked diagonally on Urbanna streets in the early days of automobiles. (Courtesy of Richard Marshall.)

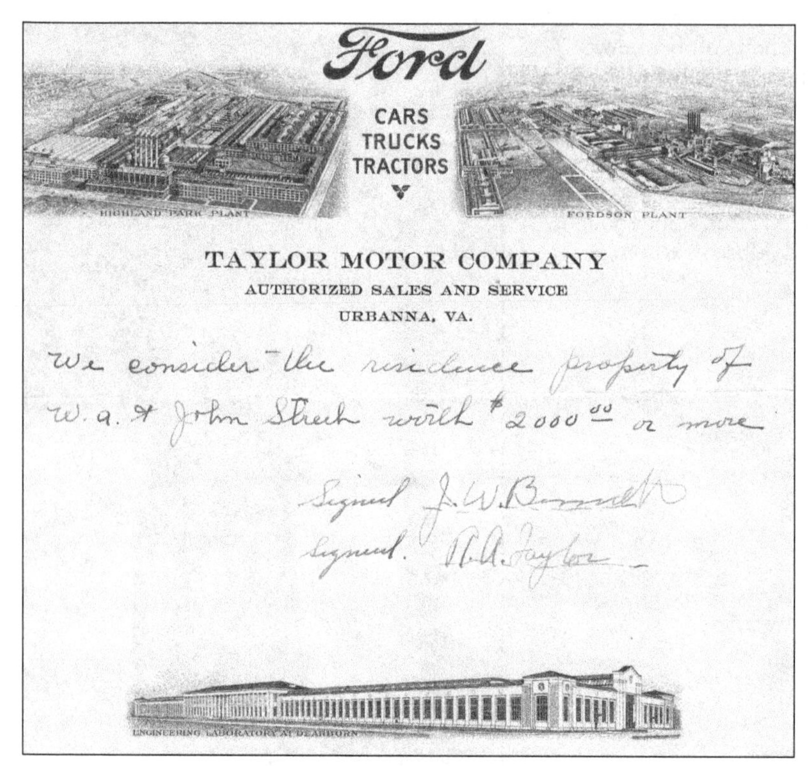
Ford

CARS
TRUCKS
TRACTORS

HIGHLAND PARK PLANT

FORDSON PLANT

TAYLOR MOTOR COMPANY

AUTHORIZED SALES AND SERVICE

URBANNA, VA.

We consider the residence property of W. A. & John Street worth $2000.00 or more

Signed J. W. B[illegible]

Signed. R. A. Taylor

ENGINEERING LABORATORY AT DEARBORN

Taylor Motor Company, owned by R. Atwill Taylor, was a well-known Ford dealership that operated on Virginia Street. Atwill's son Dickie was handicapped, and a motorized wheelchair was made for him. His warm smile and gentle nature was a wonderful part of Urbanna life. (Courtesy of Emily Chowning.)

The Swirly Top Drive-in eatery at the foot of Watling Street was the main hangout of teenagers in the 1950s. The food was served from the main building and could be eaten in the small tent to the right. In the summertime, milkshakes, banana splits, and ice cream sodas were bestsellers. (Courtesy of Bob and Carolyn Henkel.)

Six

EDUCATION

Early Colonial gentry who settled in the Urbanna area sent their children back to England to be educated. Ralph Wormeley II of Rosegill graduated from Oriel College in England in 1665 and Christopher Robinson of Hewick finished there in 1721. Ralph Wormeley III graduated from Trinity College in 1757.

In 1685, William Gordon left 100 acres near Town Bridge Road for "free school land" in his will. The first public school for the poor was built on Gordon's land around 1691. In 1764, James Reid left a lot for a school for the poor. The Palmer School, a one-room private antebellum school on Watling Street, was built in the 1840s and still stands today. Pine Grove School, later called Town Bridge School, was a public school started in 1881 for black children. Green Branch Academy, a two-room school, was founded about the same time for white children.

Burton School on Watling Street was founded in 1886 as a preparatory school for girls. Columbus Burton hired cousin Ada Walker to teach his daughters and other young ladies in a two-room school he built overlooking the creek. Private schools were conducted in the courthouse, customhouse, tobacco warehouse, and homes. Urbanna Academy, also called the Masonic School, was held in the Masonic lodge in the 1890s. The state-of-the-art, two-story, brick Urbanna High School was built in 1909 for white boys and girls. Christchurch School for boys was founded in 1921. Urbanna High School became a grade school in the 1920s and operated until 1962, when elementary schools in Middlesex County were consolidated. Urbanna tore down the 1909 schoolhouse in 1972.

Known as the Palmer School, this one-room school on Watling Street was started by Alfred Palmer in the late 1840s to educate his two children, Edmonia and Charles. He hired a teacher and allowed children in the neighborhood to attend. The Palmer School building still stands today. (Courtesy of William C. Hight.)

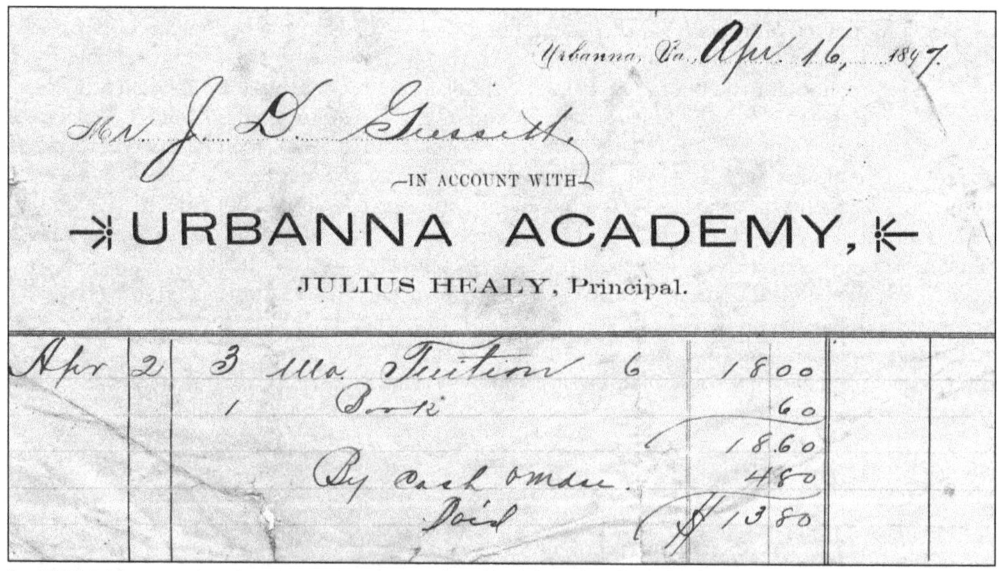

Urbanna, Va., Apr. 16, 1897.

Mr. J. D. Gressett

IN ACCOUNT WITH

URBANNA ACADEMY,

JULIUS HEALY, Principal.

Apr	2	3 Mo. Tuition	6	18 00
		1 Book		60
				18 60
		By cash order		4 80
		Paid		$13 80

In 1897, Urbanna Academy was a private school held in the three-story Masonic lodge on Watling Street. Julius Healy was principal. Parent J.D. Gressett paid $18 for three months tuition and 60¢ for each book. (Courtesy of Middlesex County Public Library.)

These students attended Green Branch Academy, a two-room school located on a branch of Perkins Creek, just west of town. The school closed in 1909 when Urbanna High and Grade School opened for white students, and those living in the vicinity. (Courtesy of Emily Chowning.)

Town builder E. Sidney Muire built Urbanna High School in 1909. It was still a high school in 1921, when students and teachers posed for this photograph in front of the school. Students went through 11th grade. (Courtesy of Burton Leaf.)

Urbanna High School was never accredited, and it was not a high school for very long. Later, the school was known as Urbanna Grade School. With grades one through six, the school remained in operation until midterm of 1962, when the county began consolidating elementary schools in expectation of the Civil Rights Act of 1964. (Courtesy of the Middlesex County Public Library.)

By 1925, Urbanna High School had become Urbanna Grade School, as noted by the chalkboard visible in this school photograph. In those days, bare feet were allowed in school. (Courtesy of Burton Leaf.)

Mrs. Billie Morgan's first-grade class at Urbanna Grade School poses for this 1937 photograph. These children started school in the thick of the Great Depression. The Depression naturally impacted the community, but unlike the Midwest and other areas of the country, the river and creek provided a year-round seafood supply that kept families from having to stand in food lines. (Courtesy of L.M. and Albert Carlton.)

Pictured here in the 1930s, students pose on May Day at Urbanna Grade School. The tradition of maypole dances went back to the days of Urbanna academies. The annual event was held on a school day as close as possible to May 1. The last maypole dance was held at Urbanna School in 1961. (Courtesy of Emily Chowning.)

The annual maypole dance was an exciting part of May Day celebrations. In this 1953 photograph, students, teachers, parents, and friends come to the annual community event. Younger students longed for the day they would be in the sixth grade and could dance around the maypole. It was one of those coming of age events for young girls and boys—part of growing up in Urbanna. For some, it was one of those innocent moments that would later give way to the songs of Elvis Presley and the Warner Drive-In Theater in the 1950s. (Courtesy of Mary Kay Hight.)

Christchurch School, a private college preparatory school, was founded in 1921. The Urbanna Board of Trade encouraged the Episcopal Diocese to locate the all-boys school near Urbanna. When the diocese decided to locate east of town, the board of trade gave a donation of $4,200 to help the school get started. (Courtesy of Middlesex County Public Library.)

Christchurch School was built on the Eastman Farm next door to the Colonial Christ Church. Before the Eastman property was purchased, townspeople tried to persuade the diocese to purchase the Urbanna Manufacturing Co. property for the school. (Courtesy of Middlesex County Public Library.)

Pulitzer Prize winning authors William Styron (*Confessions of Nat Turner*) and Lewis Puller Jr. (*Fortunate Son*) both graduated from Christchurch School. Puller also attended Urbanna Grade School. Vincent Canby also graduated from Christchurch and went on to become the chief film critic for the *New York Times.* (Courtesy of Middlesex County Public Library.)

Christchurch boys learned to sail Hampton One Design sailboats and competed in races on Urbanna Creek sponsored by the Urbanna Yacht Club. The club, founded in 1939, hosted the Hampton One Design National Championships in 1948. Club member Lloyd Emory had won the trophy the year before, which brought the championships to Urbanna. The club moved in 1949 and was renamed Fishing Bay Yacht Club. (Courtesy of Roy Bowman.)

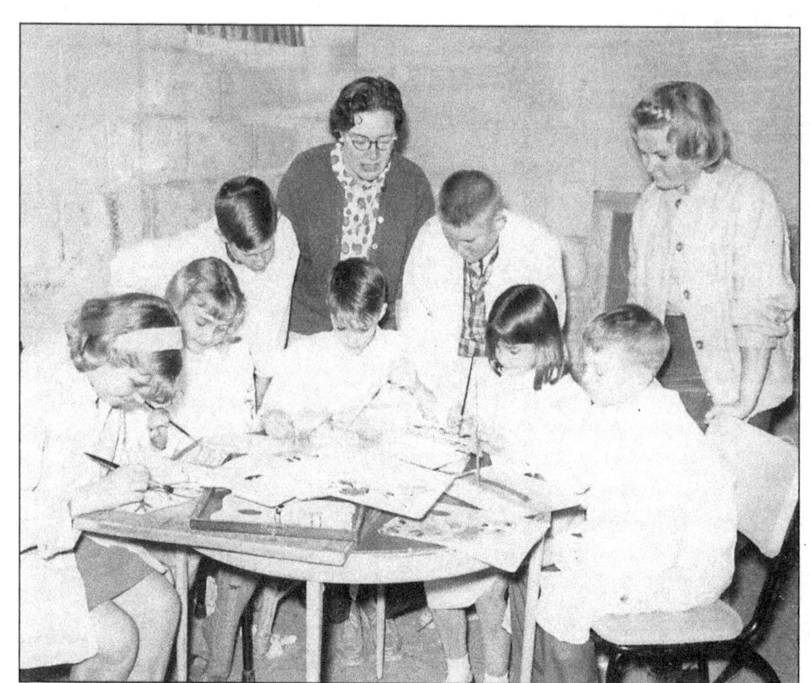

Although art had been taught in Urbanna School in the 1940s by artist Mary Burton, art was not taught in public schools in the early 1960s. In response, local artists Isabel French and Emily Chowning held art classes for local children in Chowning's basement on Watling Street. (Courtesy of Emily Chowning.)

Pictured the year the school was founded, these students attended Urbanna Nursery School in 1957. The school, founded by Terry Taylor and Emily Chowning, was held in a basement of a home on Watling Street. When public schools initiated kindergarten classes in the 1970s, these types of schools closed. (Courtesy of Emily Chowning.)

In the 1950s and 1960s, there were no YMCA summer camps. The Urbanna Baptist and Methodist churches both held summer Bible schools attended by Baptist, Methodist, and Episcopalian children. These students attended bible school at the Urbanna Baptist Church in 1950s. (Courtesy of Emily Chowning.)

Blitz, a Chesapeake Bay Retriever, attended Urbanna Baptist Bible School for several summers, arriving daily with his master. Minister Fred Billups distributed this photograph to each child in the late 1950s, saying Blitz was the most dedicated attendee of the school. (Courtesy of Emily Chowning.)

The opening of the Urbanna Bible School in 1960 was the start of a turbulent decade in Urbanna and Middlesex County. In the early 1960s, federal law mandated integration. Ministers in white and black churches worked together to pave a smooth transition. Minister Fred Billups encouraged his congregation to cast off prejudice and accept integration. (Courtesy of Emily Chowning.)

A boy and his dog learned of life together. They shaped footprints in winter snow, on shallow water mud flats in spring, on sandy beaches in summer, and through autumn leaves in the fall. Together, they conquered "Jimmy" crabs, fiddler crabs, grey trout, and stiff-back perch as ospreys, eagles, kingfishers, and ducks flew across their world. (Courtesy of Emily Chowning.)

Seven

Churches, Streets, and Bridges

From the beginning, religion has been a guiding force in Urbanna. The first church was the Anglican Christ Church founded in 1666, located several miles outside of town. Urbanna is etched in Virginia Baptist history as one of the towns that imprisoned Baptist minister John Waller for preaching the gospel without a license. In 1771, James Montague arrested Waller and threw him and several of his disciples in the Urbanna jail. Waller preached from the jail window and won hundreds of followers.

Pioneer Methodist minister George Whitefield arrived in town in 1763, and Bishop Francis Asbury came in 1785. Both came and left with little fanfare. When the Middlesex County Courthouse was moved from Urbanna to Saluda, the Colonial courthouse building in town was converted in 1852 to a nondenominational church. The church was used by early Baptists, Methodists, and Episcopalians. In 1896, the Methodists bought the courthouse/church, where they worshiped until 1902, when a new Methodist church was built. Urbanna Baptist church was built in 1895. During the 1950s and 1960s, Catholics held Mass in the Rappanna Theater and later, at the Urbanna Fire House.

Streets were dirt roads for most of the town's history. The roads were paved in the 1940s after the state of Virginia took over the highway system. The first bridge across the creek was built in 1859 by the Urbanna Toll Bridge Company. There were three wooden bridges across Urbanna Creek before a concrete bridge was completed in 1957.

When the courthouse was moved from Urbanna to Saluda, John and Eliza Bailey of Rosegill bought the building in 1852 and converted it into a nondenominational church. Methodists bought it in 1896. In 1907, the building was converted to an Episcopal chapel. Today, the structure is owned by the Middlesex County Women's Club and is used as a church for denominations without facilities. (Courtesy of Emily Chowning.)

Urbanna Baptist Church was built in 1895 by Charles Henry Palmer Sr. A Civil War veteran, Palmer left his hometown of Urbanna in 1865 and went to New York state, where he took up carpentry. He came home seven years later and built the church, the Masonic lodge, and several homes using a Folk Victorian style with an Italianate influence, which he had learned in New York. (Courtesy of Emily Chowning.)

Deacons and women leaders of Urbanna Baptist Church gather in front of the church in this 1940s photograph. Women's church groups were an early platform that led to the women's movement. Through the church, women took leadership roles involving temperance, mission work, and other social issues. Church leadership roles aided women in realizing they could be a positive force in society. (Courtesy of Emily Chowning.)

The side wings on the Urbanna Baptist church were added by builder and architect Charles Palmer in 1904. This was one of the last major works Palmer completed, as he died in December 1905. The church, along with several other buildings constructed and designed by the Civil War veteran, is listed in *Buildings of Virginia*, published by the Society of Architectural Historians. (Courtesy of Kevin Barrick.)

All Quotations are Subject to Immediate Acceptance.

A. D. ALEXANDER,

PATENTEE AND SOLE MANUFACTURER OF

All Agreements are Contingent Upon Strikes, Accidents, or Other Delays Unavoidable or Beyond our Control.

ALEXANDER'S EXCELSIOR PACKING PADS AND WRAPPERS.

URBANNA, VA. Nov 5th/08.

Mr J.D.Gressitt.

Dear Brother:-

Enclosed you will find check $7.55 to balance a/c of The Urbanna Baptist Church painting bill.

Yours very truly,

805
Less 50 donated
$7.55

C.A. Hotchkins
Church Treas

C.A. Hotchkins, treasurer of Urbanna Baptist Church in 1908, was associated with Urbanna's A.D. Alexander, a firm that made excelsior packing pads and wrappers. He used this invoice to confirm to J.D. Gressitt that a balance of $7.55 had been paid for painting the church. (Courtesy of Middlesex County Public Library.)

Nannie Sadler Palmer was a charter member of Urbanna Baptist Church. Palmer lived by strict 18th century Baptist rules. She preached no drinking, no dancing, and no profane language. Neighbor Maggie Hoge, who made communion wine for Christ Episcopal Church, constantly agitated her. Palmer referred to Episcopalians as "whiskeypalians." (Courtesy of Emily Chowning.)

This c. 1905 postcard of Watling Street shows the recently built Urbanna Baptist Church and the three-story Masonic lodge in the distance. (Courtesy of Emily Chowning.)

Methodist bishop Francis Asbury visited Urbanna in 1785 and 1800. On his second trip, he sent word ahead that he was coming to preach in the town courthouse building. He wrote, "the courthouse doors were open but not one soul appeared." The Methodist faith did eventually grow, and in 1902, this brick church was built on the corner of Prince George and Cross Streets. (Courtesy of Middlesex County Public Library.)

This early 20th century photograph shows the recently built Methodist Church on Prince George Street. The first *Southside Sentinel* newspaper office, founded in 1896, was located in a building on Prince George Street. Allen Group now occupies the location, known by longtime residents as "the old Methodist Church parsonage lot." (Courtesy of Emily Chowning.)

This photograph shows the back of the Urbanna Masonic lodge at the corner of Watling and Cross Streets. The building was used as a church by Urbanna's Methodist congregations for a number of years. The wooden lodge on the left was completed around 1877. A home at the end of Watling Street was used for veterans of the Civil War. (Courtesy of Emily Chowning.)

INDEPENDENT ORDER OF ODD FELLOWS
Official Certificate

$ 10.0 July 20 1912

This Certifies that Bro.
WHOSE SIGNATURE APPEARS IN THE MARGIN HEREOF
HAS PAID
To URBANNA. LODGE No. 79 I.O.O.F.
of URBANNA. Jurisdiction of Va
the sum of One 100 Dollars
in full for all charges to Sept 30 1912
EXCEPT ASSESSMENTS LEVIED AFTER THE DATE OF THIS CERTIFICATE.
SEAL
No. 9
NOT IN FORCE AFTER DATE CANCELLED SECRETARY
JAN. FEB. MAR. APRIL MAY JUNE JULY AUG. SEPT. OCT. NOV. DEC.
1912. 1913. 1914. 1915. 1916. 1917. 1918. 1919. 1920. 1921. 1922. 1923.
Signature of Holder

The Independent Order of Odd Fellows (IOOF) Urbanna Lodge No. 79 operated out of the old Masonic lodge for a number of years. The IOOF paid rent to the Masons to use the second floor of the lodge. (Courtesy of Middlesex County Public Library.)

Concrete sidewalks were laid in 1941 in front of what is now Nimcock Gallery on Cross Street. Next to the gallery is the "Old Regal Building," today the Urbanna Town Hall. Next to the town hall, Taylor Hardware Store was in operation then. (Courtesy of Dick Murray.)

This 1941 photograph shows the old Texaco station at the corner of Cross and Virginia Streets and some major roadwork underway, as the town and the United States were preparing for World War II. (Courtesy of Dick Murray.)

No. 1.—Urbanna Bridge, Va.

Several years after a county voting referendum successfully moved the Middlesex County Courthouse from Urbanna to Saluda in 1852, the Urbanna Creek Toll Bridge Company was founded to build a bridge across Urbanna Creek. (Courtesy of Emily Chowning.)

The first toll bridge across Urbanna Creek was owned by a group of local stockholders. James H. Hackney was the first president of the group, and William S. Christian, Alfred Palmer, and Edward T. Purkins were appointed to frame a constitution and bylaws. (Courtesy of Buddy Davis.)

This was the last wooden bridge across Urbanna Creek from Rosegill to Urbanna. It was replaced in 1957 by a modern concrete bridge that is still in use today. (Courtesy of Middlesex County Public Library.)

The wooden bridge across Urbanna Creek is seen here in the early 1950s. Outside barbecue pits complete with brick chimneys were in just about every backyard in those days, as outside cooking grills were soon to become the norm. (Courtesy of Terry Murphy.)

The modern Urbanna Bridge was completed and dedicated in 1957. Walker Jones, daughter of Middlesex County commonwealth attorney Lewis Jones Jr. and his wife Laura, cut the ribbon as hundreds of bystanders looked on. Shortly after the dedication, the wooden bridge across the creek was torn down. (Courtesy of Terry Murphy.)

Eight

PEOPLE

The most famous person to live and own property in Urbanna was Revolutionary War diplomat Arthur Lee, who lived at Lansdowne. Dr. John Mitchell lived in town in the 1740s. Besides being a physician, he was a botanist and a mapmaker. He is known as the man who made the "Map of the British and French Dominion," often considered the most important map in American history. The map was published in 1755 and used by English and America officials at Paris in 1782 and 1783 in negotiating the treaty that terminated the Revolutionary War.

For many years, a plaque hung on the wall of the Gressitt House on Virginia Street commemorating William Clark's departure from this house in 1803 to join Meriwether Lewis for the Lewis and Clark expedition westward. In 1913 William Jennings Bryan, a three-time Democratic candidate for the presidency of the United States, came to town and spoke on the grounds of Urbanna Baptist Church.

Over more than 300 years, the town has seen many, many faces of those who have lived in and visited Urbanna. There have been young and old, strong and weak, black and white, and good and evil. Faces come and go, but Urbanna remains a small waterfront town perched upon high banks.

Urbanna Masonic Lodge #83 was organized in 1872. This early 1900s photograph shows the many faces involved in the lodge when the building was located on the corner of Watling and Cross Streets. (Courtesy of Urbanna Masonic Lodge #83.)

Farmer James Henry Chowning appears in this late 1800s photograph. He lived at the Glebe at the head of Urbanna Creek. (Courtesy of Betty Chowning.)

The Street family lived on Watling Street in what became the Urbanna Baptist Church parsonage. Pictured are, from left to right, (seated) sisters Miss Lizzie Sadler and Mary Street; (standing) Mary's children John, Annette, and W.A. Street. (Courtesy of Emily Chowning.)

These children play on a wagon in the summertime. (Courtesy of L.M. and Albert Carlton.)

Family gatherings often centered around the family's oyster boat. On Saturdays in spring and summer after oyster tongs are put aside, hand-lines for bottom fishing were pulled out. Family members of all ages went along for a day of fishing, often resulting in lifelong memories. (Courtesy of Betty Shelton.)

After church on some Sunday afternoons, picnics were held on the high banks of Urbanna Creek to raise funds for the church. This photograph was taken in the early 1900s of members of the Burton, Palmer, Street, Chowning, and Sadler families attending one of those affairs. (Courtesy of Emily Chowning.)

Members of the Heath family pose for a photograph at their home. In the late 1800s, George Heath operated a store and an "oyster shanty town." During the winter, oystermen came to Urbanna from surrounding counties to harvest oysters. Heath's little shanties provided shelter for men and boys. (Courtesy of L. M. and Albert Carlton.)

John Street grew up to be a giant of a man. His gentle spirit was highly regarded. As an adult, Street worked for the town ice plant, delivering blocks of ice door-to-door in a wheelbarrow. (Courtesy of Emily Chowning.)

Oysterman McKinley "Mac" Wilson supplemented his income by making hickory oyster mops used to scrub down oyster boats. (Author's collection.)

This man is holding a horseshoe crab on the dock at J.W. Hurley & Son Seafood. Many in the black community owned their own oyster boats and worked for themselves. Others found work in the town's seafood business as oystermen, crabbers, fishermen, oyster shuckers, shell movers, dock workers, and mates and cooks aboard schooners. (Courtesy of Grace Daniel.)

The wooden boat builder was part of the local oyster culture. Throughout town history, boats were built along the shore of Urbanna Creek. Above, Tom Trevilian is building a deadrise boat. Note the stem is lowered into a "stem hole" dug in the ground so the hull can be built "upside down" on an even level. Trevilain was the last wooden oyster boat builder in town. He built 42-foot deadrise workboats in his backyard on the corner of Howard Street and Rappahannock Avenue. The 1964 photograph below shows a young boy using the upside down hull as a playground. (Courtesy of Joe Conboy.)

Steamed "Jimmy" crabs are sweet summer fare. Here Mary Burton and a friend are "chicken necking" off a pier in front of their house on Urbanna Creek in the 1930s. A ball of string with a chicken neck or fish head tied to the end has lured many a crab from the sea into a boiling pot. (Courtesy of Betty Burton.)

Crab nets and wooden skiffs have been a part of town culture for generations. These youngsters are taking a break from catching soft-shell crabs in the 1920s. Fried soft shells are a local delicacy to this day. (Courtesy of L. M. and Albert Carlton.)

Richard and Tommy Marshall pose on the engine cabin of a Chesapeake Bay log canoe in the early 1930s. Boats made of three and five logs were used to harvest oysters on the Rappahannock River. (Courtesy of Richard Marshall.)

The automobile was still a relatively new phenomenon in 1930. Running boards that kept mud off the body of the vehicle were standard equipment on cars then. They also provided a platform for this young lad to pose for a photograph. (Courtesy of Emily Chowning.)

The footbridge over Perkins Creek was a good summertime crabbing spot. Pictured here around 1950, "Little" Bill Hight was ready and willing to catch a big "Jimmy" crab. (Courtesy of Joe Cardwell.)

Here, a couple of soft-shell crabs have been caught. (Courtesy of William C. Hight.)

For summertime play in the 1930s, cousins Shep Chowning and Catherine Jones went swimming in Urbanna Creek. For generations, the creek has provided high quality of life, economically, socially, and esthetically. (Courtesy of Emily Chowning.)

This early 1950s photograph shows "summertime on a stick." Ruth Christian Hight poses for a photograph while her brother Bill is armed with a crab net on the Rappahannock River. (Courtesy of William C. Hight.)

Over the years, recreational fishing has brought many anglers to Urbanna. Here, two men hold a string of trophy fish in front of little Richard Marshall in the early 1930s. Fishing season is year round on the river. Saltwater trout, croaker, spot, bluefish, and perch are caught in the warmer months, and rockfish are landed in the fall and winter. (Courtesy of Richard Marshall.)

This cownose ray was caught on light tackle in Rappahannock River in 1958 and hung on a pole so photographs could be taken of it. (Courtesy of Emily Chowning.)

Recreational boating grew in popularity after World War II. Some families owned little boats with outboard motors to go for a Saturday "bottom" fishing trip. (Courtesy of Joe Cardwell.)

The first automobiles arrived in town around 1911 via steamboat from Baltimore. This boy sits on top of an early "horseless carriage." (Courtesy of Richard Marshall.)

Dr. Thomas F. Marshall Sr. is seen here on the day an early telephone booth was installed in his drug store. (Courtesy of Richard Marshall.)

Once, a state trooper caught a drunk man staggering home from a poker game. The trooper was about to write a ticket for public drunkenness when town constable Willie Buck arrived. Buck talked the trooper out of it, saying, "I don't write them tickets. I take them home safe and sound." When Willie Buck died there was standing room only in the church. (Courtesy of Richard Marshall.)

The era of semipro baseball was a golden age in town history, and pre–World War II teams brought excitement and pride to the community. By the end of the 1940s, however, television brought baseball into the living rooms of townsfolk, and the community team folded. (Courtesy of Bonnie Williams.)

Hard-throwing pitcher Jock Bristow was a player and coach for the Urbanna semipro baseball team in the 1940s. Once the team traveled to Norfolk to play and Urbanna had as its pitcher a young man from Norfolk. When the team arrived, Norfolk fans yelled, "you had to get a pitcher from Norfolk to come play us." Bristow changed the lineup, pitched himself, and Urbanna won the game. (Courtesy of Bonnie Williams.)

Players on Urbanna's 1930s and 1940s baseball teams were roll-up-your-sleeves, hard-playing, blue-collar boys who loved baseball, and the fans loved them. During home games, charter-boat captains advertised that charters were only a half day, in order to get back to watch the local team play. (Courtesy of Bonnie Williams.)

The Burch twins Lewis and Stanley played outfield for Urbanna. Fans used to say that if a batter hit a ball to one of the Burch twins it was like hitting it in a tar barrel. It stuck in the glove every time. (Courtesy of Bonnie Williams.)

Before swimming pools, the Urbanna Beach was lined with people sunbathing in the sand, while others swam, dove from the diving platform, and played water games. The public beach was netted to keep out the pesky stinging nettles and had a manned lifeguard stand on shore. (Courtesy of Beatrice Taylor.)

Henry Lee McMann poses near his home with his nephew Joe Cardwell on Taylor Avenue. Originally from Tangier Island, McMann moved to Urbanna after the "August Storm" of 1933. The hurricane brought seas that rose into the second stories of island homes. Thirteen Tangier families moved lock, stock, and barrel by boat to the town they called Banna. (Courtesy of Joe Cardwell.)

Millionaire Willis Sharpe Kilmer came to town in 1909 from Binghampton, New York, and built this 32-room Tudor mansion on a 1,000-acre farm just outside of town. The family made a fortune with a patent medicine called Dr. Kilmer's Swamp Root. Soon after Kilmer arrived, West Urbanna Wharf was renamed Remlik Wharf. Remlik is Kilmer spelled backwards. (Courtesy of *Southside Sentinel.*)

Kilmer's mansion mysteriously burned in 1938. Remlik Hall Farm employed many people from town. Some remember caring for Kilmer's famous racehorses Exterminator, Sun Briar, and Sunbeau. Exterminator was the 1918 winner of the Kentucky Derby and was named Horse of the Year in 1921. (Courtesy of the Stanley Hart family.)

Nine

Early Festivals

Over the years, town businesses and the Urbanna Boosters Club tried to stimulate the economy by holding events. One of the more successful was the Labor Day Regatta boat race. The event was sponsored by the Boosters Club and the Middlesex County Lions Club, featuring outboard and inboard hydroplanes. The outboard races were held on Sunday, and the inboards were held on Monday. Labor Day boat races started in 1940 and ended in 1966.

In 1958, members of the Boosters Club decided to hold an event called Urbanna Day. The first Urbanna Day drew 5,000 people. A parade was held, and town businesses sponsored raffles and sales. It was held for the next three years. On September 28, 1961, the headline in the *Southside Sentinel* read, "Urbanna Day Grows into the Urbanna Oyster Festival." The oyster fishery was still a vital part of Urbanna's economy.

The first festival drew several thousand people from surrounding towns. As the word spread, the festival continued to grow and in the 1980s, attendance soared as 60,000-plus people came to Urbanna. The festival features two parades, the state-champion oyster-shucking contest, and the queens contest. There is also an education day held on Thursday, when schoolchildren learn about the history and origin of the oyster, and oysters and seafood prepared in every way imaginable. In 1988, the Virginia General Assembly voted to make the Urbanna Oyster Festival the official oyster festival of the commonwealth of Virginia.

The "Labor Day Regatta" was held from 1940 to 1966, when safety concerns over high-speed boats ended the event. Each year before the races, a boat parade was held with "flower garlanded yachts and boats." (Courtesy of Richard Marshall.)

The hydroplane pits were busy when the outboard races were held on Labor Day Sunday. (Courtesy of Anne Wheeley.)

Teenage girls drive a flock of Remlik Hall Farm turkeys down Cross Street in 1951. It was part a Thanksgiving "short" film by Movie-time News that appeared in theaters around the country. Afterwards, a turkey race was held in the middle of the street. (Courtesy of Richard Marshall.)

At the fourth annual Urbanna Day, the Richmond Region Association of the Antique Automobile Club of America brought their cars. The town favorite was a red 1915 Ford owned by Harold Taylor, the town plumber. (Courtesy of *Southside Sentinel.*)

The first Little Miss Spat competition started in 1966. Pictured here are some of the first Little Miss Spat contestants. (Courtesy of *Southside Sentinel.*)

The parade route came down Cross Street in 1966. A military marching band was part of the event. (Courtesy of *Southside Sentinel.*)

The "Queen and her Court" was an annual parade float. (Courtesy of *Southside Sentinel.*)

Julie Marshall was crowned the 1967 Urbanna Oyster Festival Queen. The 1966 queen, Barbara Davis, places the crown on her head. (Courtesy of *Southside Sentinel.*)

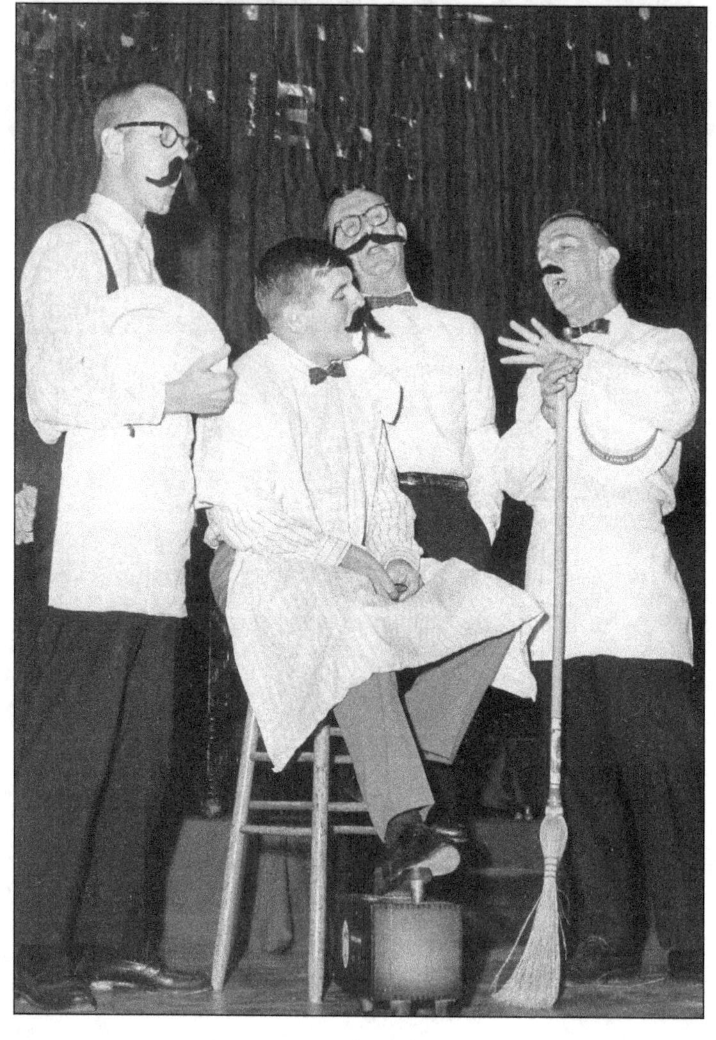

By the 1970s, the crowds were growing at the annual Urbanna Oyster Festival. In just a few short years, over 60,000 people would attend the annual festival in November. (Courtesy of *Southside Sentinel.*)

A show held on the Rappanna Theater stage at the 1966 Oyster Festival featured this barbershop quartet featuring Roger Hopper, Aubrey Hall, Al Miller, and Bob Barlowe. (Courtesy of *Southside Sentinel.*)

The Oyster Festival queen contestants at the 1968 festival sang and tap danced into the hearts of all those attending. (Courtesy of *Southside Sentinel.*)

In 1968, Oyster Festival royalty featured queen Pat Thrift and Emma Jean Williams, Little Miss Spat. Thrift was crowned by 1967 queen Joyce Bowen. Williams was crowned by 1967 Little Miss Spat Karen Strickland. (Courtesy of *Southside Sentinel.*)

Since the town was formed, Urbanna Creek has played a dynamic role in Urbanna life. Hundreds of people came by water during the Urbanna Oyster Festival. For those living in town, the creek and Rappahannock River have been the lifeblood of the community. Whether in the era of tobacco, oysters, or today's tourist trade, the water has touched the lives of each and every one who has been fortunate to call Urbanna their home. (Courtesy of *Southside Sentinel.*)

INDEX

Bibliography

Drolshagen, Mardie and Edward J. Petuch. *Molluscan Paleontology of the Chesapeake Miocene.* Boca Raton, London, New York: Taylor & Francis Group, 2010.

Gray, Louise E. *Historic Buildings in Middlesex County Virginia, 1650–1875.* Charlotte, NC: Delmar Printing Co., 1978.

Heads of Families First Census of the United States: 1790—State Enumerations of Virginia: From 1782 to 1785. Baltimore, MD: Southern Book Co., 1952.

Holly, David C. *Tidewater By Steamboat: A Saga of the Chesapeake.* Baltimore and London: Johns Hopkins University Press, 1991.

Laing, Wesley Newton. "Report On A Building At Urbanna Virginia." Association for the Preservation Of Virginia Antiquities, prepared under the general direction of the Ralph Wormeley Chapter and a special committee for APVA, 1958–1960.

Mason, George Carrington. "Tobacco Coast: A Maritime History of Chesapeake Bay in the Colonial Era." *Newport News,* 1953.

Middlesex Court Order Book, 1682–1710.

Nugent, Nell Marion. *Cavaliers and Pioneers: Abstracts of Virginia Land Patents and Grants 1623–1800.* Richmond, VA: Press of the Dietz Printing Co., 1934.

O'Sullivan, Richard O. *55th Virginia Infantry.* Lynchburg, VA: H.E. Howard Inc., 1989.

Roundtree, Helen C. *Pocahontas's People: The Powhatan Indians of Virginia Through Four Centuries.* Norman, OK: University of Oklahoma Press, 1990.

Ryland, Evelyn Q. *Urbanna: A Port Town in Virginia 1680–1980.* Charlotte, NC: Delmar Printing Co., 1980.

Beale, Rev. G.W. *A History of the Rise and Progress of the Baptists in Virginia,* rev. ed. Pitt & Publishers, 1894.

Slaughter, James B. *Settlers, Southerners, Americans: The History of Essex County, Virginia, 1608–1984.* Waynesville, NC: Don Mills Inc., 1985.

Taylor, Chas A. *A History of Urbanna Lodge No. 83 A.F. & A.M.* Urbanna Lodge, 1959.

CPSIA information can be obtained
at www.ICGtesting.com
Printed in the USA
LVHW021035171022
730847LV00002B/150

9 781531 662394